There are more than 195,289 regi   itutions in the UK that spend close to £80 b   there are another 191,000 charities that don'ı

According to a charity regulatory b ɔ, unese charities make a huge thirteen billion 'asks' for donations every year – that's around two hundred 'asks' for every man, woman and child in the UK.

Britain's registered charities claim that almost ninety pence in every pound we give them is spent on what they call 'charitable activities'. But with many of our best-known charities, the real figure is likely to be less than fifty pence in every pound. With too many charities, at least half of our money goes on management, administration, strategy development, political campaigning and fundraising – not on what most of us would consider 'good causes'.

But does Britain really need so many charities? And do our charities spend enough of our money on good causes?

Or is there a massive amount of waste with sometimes five, ten, fifteen or even more registered charities all covering roughly the same areas, yet all with their own executives, administrators, fundraisers, communications experts, advertising campaigns, awareness programmes, offices, computers, fancy logos, colourful reports and so on and so forth?

The British public are becoming increasingly concerned over the way that charities raise and use the tens of billions we give them.

The Great Charity Scandal exposes the truth about Britain's massive charity industry, revealing how our money is really spent, and shows what needs to be done so that much more of the money we donate to charity actually does get used in the way we expect.

David Craig spent most of his career selling and running sales training courses for some of the world's best and worst management consultancies. After writing two whistleblowing books, ***Rip-Off*** and ***Plundering the Public Sector***, about how consultants take millions from businesses and government departments while delivering little of value, he was blacklisted and so left the profession.

Since then he has written several books exposing government corruption, incompetence, stupidity and waste, including ***Squandered*** *How Gordon Brown is wasting over one trillion pounds of our money* and ***Fleeced*** *How we've been betrayed by politicians, bureaucrats and bankers*, both of which won the Hammond Whiteley journalism award.

He is also the author of:

The Great European Rip-Off

Pillaged! *How they're looting £413 million a day from your savings and pensions*

Greed Unlimited *How Cameron and Clegg protect the elites while squeezing the rest of us*

Don't Buy It! *Tricks and Traps Salespeople Use and How to Beat Them*

Who Cares? *One family's shocking story of 'care' in today's NHS (with Amanda Steane)*

Praise for *Squandered*

"This is a terrifying book, but a brilliant and necessary one…Please read it." *Daily Telegraph*

"The most illuminating political book to date this year." *Evening Standard*

"Prepare to weep." *Daily Telegraph*

"Impossible to read without becoming angry." *New Statesman*

Praise for *Plundering the Public Sector*

"This is a good topic and Craig knows his stuff. He writes with passionate disgust and with rich detail." *Management Today*

"The first serious book to deal in a thorough fashion with the incompetence, nepotism and waste that have defined New Labour in government." *Spectator*

"Racy yet well-researched….gripping and important." *New Statesman*

Praise for *Rip-Off*

"The most shocking book of the year." *Independent on Sunday*

THE GREAT CHARITY SCANDAL

What really happens to the billions we give to good causes?

David Craig

Original Book Company

The Original Book Company
Unit E2, Kings Walk,
19a Knyveton Road,
Bournemouth BH1 3QZ

www.snouts-in-the-trough.com
email: originalbookco@yahoo.co.uk

First published in the UK by The Original Book Company

A copy of the British Library Cataloguing in Publication Data is available from the British Library

ISBN: 978-1872188119
Written, printed and bound in the EU

Contents

Introduction

2. 50

The need for this book

The figures are astonishing. There are more than 195,289 registered charities and charitable institutions in the UK that raise and spend close to £80 billion a year. Plus there are another 191,000 charities that don't need to register, either due to legal exemptions or because they raise less than £5,000 a year. And the Charity Commission receives around twenty five new applications for charitable status every single working day.

These more than 195,289 registered charities employ over one million staff. That's one charity employee for every sixty people living in Britain. There are three times as many staff employed in Britain's registered charities than there are in the military and the police put together. Five times as many people work for charities, the so-called 'voluntary sector', than run our railways providing four million journeys a day, about one and a half billion journeys a year. Charity is one of Britain's biggest industries – larger than our car, aerospace and chemical sectors. In addition, there are well over a million charity trustees who don't get salaries, but who can all claim expenses from the money we donate.

According to a charity regulatory body, these charities make a huge thirteen billion 'asks' for money every year – that's around two hundred 'asks' for every man, woman and child in the UK.

Britain's registered charities claim that almost ninety pence in every pound we give them is spent on what they call 'charitable activities'. But with many of our best-known charities, the real figure is likely to be less than fifty pence in every pound. With too many charities, at least half of our money goes on management, administration, strategy development, political campaigning and fundraising – not on what most of us would consider 'good causes'.

But does Britain really need so many charities? And do we need so many people working for charities? Or is there a massive amount of waste with sometimes five, ten, fifteen or even more registered charities all covering roughly the same areas, yet all with their own executives, administrators, fundraisers, communications experts, advertising campaigns, awareness programmes, offices, computers, fancy logos, colourful reports and so on and so forth?

The British public are becoming increasingly concerned over the way that charities raise and use the tens of billions we donate. *The Great Charity Scandal* exposes the truth about Britain's massive charity industry, revealing how our money is really spent, and shows what needs to be done so that much more of the money we give to charity actually does get used in the way we expect.

Chapter 1

A Hungry Monster?

The charity industry

Some people might find the figures astonishing. There are 164,515 charities and charitable institutions approved by the £22 million-a-year Charity Commission for England and Wales. These charities raise around £63 billion a year. The £3 million-a-year Office of the Scottish Charity Regulator has counted another 23,774 in Scotland bringing in about £10 billion a year. And the recently-formed Charity Commission for Northern Ireland has started collecting details of charities there. The Northern Ireland Commission believes there are at least 7,000 charities on its patch, though the number could be as high as 12,000. But there are so many that the Northern Ireland Commission estimates it will take several years for it to register them all and thus find out how many there really are and how much money they bring in and spend.

That gives us at least 195,289 registered charities in the UK. If we assume the UK population is around sixty five million, then we have a registered charity for every 333 people living in the UK. Moreover, the Charity Commission receives around 125 new applications from organisations for charitable status every week and in just one year registered one thousand new Christian or Christian-related charities and four hundred new charities of other religious faiths.[1]

In addition there are about another 191,000 unregistered charities. Around 80,000 of these unregistered charities fall below the threshold for registration, currently set at an annual income of £5,000. Most of the remaining 111,000 unregistered charities are 'excepted charities' – charities that have previously been excepted by regulation or order with an income of £100,000 or less, such as local parish councils affiliated with the Church of England and other mainstream Christian organisations, scout and guide groups, and armed forces charities or organisations which have their own regulator such as English universities which are regulated by Higher Education Funding Council for England.

The 164,515 registered charities in England and Wales employ 897,256 paid managers and staff. In addition, there are 946,682 unpaid trustees who can claim expenses and another 3,134,803 volunteers. The Office of the Scottish Charity Regulator doesn't collate any information on the numbers of people working for their 23,774 registered charities nor on the numbers of trustees and volunteers. And, of course, in Northern Ireland it will be a few years before we even know how many charities there are, never mind the number of employees, trustees and volunteers.

If we just look at England and Wales, where we have some detailed figures, with the registered charities there is a paid charity worker for every sixty three people, a charity trustee for every sixty people and a charity volunteer for every eighteen people. So it seems we have awful lot of charitable folk concerned with our welfare, the welfare of our pets and other animals and things like the environment and poverty and so on. Moreover, these charities seem very active in seeking our financial support. With an estimated thirteen billion requests for money being made to us by charities each year, many people feel bombarded by pleas for donations to help a seemingly endless succession of deserving good causes.[2]

Do you do what I do?

With so many charities, the extent of possible duplication, triplication, quadruplication and worse amongst charities could seem truly astounding to an inexperienced outsider. Many thousands, or even tens of thousands, of charities will be worthy organisations which have been given charitable tax status due to the nature of the work they do, but which don't solicit money from us either directly in the form of donations or indirectly as government grants. These would include schools, churches, hospitals, emergency services, community groups, universities and so on. Nevertheless, just in England and Wales there are 1,939 active charities focused on children; 581 charities trying to find a cure for cancer or else help victims of cancer; 354 charities for birds; 255 charities for animals, 81 charities for people with alcohol problems and, even in a limited field like leukaemia, we have no fewer than 68 charities all eagerly asking for our money for their particular good cause. Few of these charities will admit they are doing exactly the same thing as other charities. But it possibly stretches credibility to claim that Britain really needs them all.

Quote: *Two decades ago there were thought to be 70 charities operating in Ethiopia; today the figure is close to 5,000. After any major disaster, where once 40 groups operated, there will now be in excess of 1,000, causing chaos and confusion rather than helping the afflicted, as seen following the Haitian earthquake two years ago.*[3]

Play 'Match the Charity'

When you look at the mission statements of many charities, they can start to look remarkably similar. There are probably more than a hundred charities which claim their aim is to reduce poverty. On the Charity Commission's website, these charities explain their purpose in life:

- The £368 million-a-year Oxfam declares *'Oxfam's objects are to prevent and relieve poverty and protect the vulnerable anywhere in the world'*.
- Then comes the £95 million-a-year Christian Aid where *'we work with the world's poorest people to tackle causes and consequences of poverty and campaign for change'*.
- And the £59 million-a-year ActionAid, *'ActionAid seeks to bring about positive and lasting change in the lives of the poor and socially excluded people around the world. We believe that poverty can be ended and that it can be achieved by working alongside and supporting people in poverty'*.
- Plus we have the £49 million-a-year Cafod (Catholic Agency for Overseas Development), *'Cafod works in partnership with communities in the Global South to reduce poverty and bring about sustainable change through development and humanitarian programmes. It also campaigns for social justice and an end to poverty'*.
- In addition, there's the £39 million-a-year Care International UK, *'Care International is a global charity dedicated to ending poverty. We aim for long term impact through our humanitarian and development work'*.

I could go on with War on Want – *'fights poverty in developing countries'*; World Vision - *'challenges the policies and practices that perpetuate poverty'*; Concern Worldwide – *'dedicated to ...the ultimate elimination of extreme poverty in the world's poorest countries'*, Comic Relief – *'bring about real lasting change by tackling the root causes of poverty'*

And many more, all bravely fighting to eliminate poverty and usually all operating in the same blighted countries doing similar sorts of things in their war on poverty (see Figure 1).

Figure 1 – There are remarkable similarities between the aims of six of our best-known anti-poverty charities

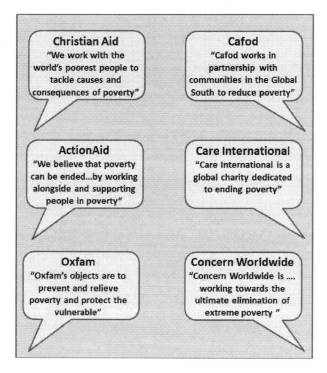

I suspect that if you took a few experts from the Charity Commission and gave them each a set of cards with the names of ten to fifteen anti-poverty charities and other cards with these charities' mission statements on them, very few of these Charity Commission experts would be able to correctly match the charity and the mission statements as these mission statements are all so similar. That then poses the question – do we need so many anti-poverty charities all with their chief executives and fundraising managers and financial directors and commercial directors and so on?

The mission statements of three prostate cancer charities also seemed to have more than a little overlap in their activities (see Figure 2)

Figure 2 – Three prostate cancer charities all appeared to be involved in similar areas – helping sufferers and funding research

Three prostate cancer charities – but can you spot the difference?

Prostate Cancer Research Foundation (a) the promotion of the study of and research into the causes of and a cure for and the relief of cancer of the prostate and similar diseases; and (b) the provision of relief and/or treatment for anyone suffering from any such ailment disease or complaint

Prostate Action has two main aims, the first to educate and train healthcare professionals in all prostate diseases; and the second to promote independent worldwide research into all aspects of prostate disease, and to spread the crucial knowledge gathered from that research as far afield as possible, via internationally recognised forum

Prostate Cancer UK fights to help more men survive prostate cancer and enjoy a better quality of life. We support men living with prostate cancer, prostate diseases and the effects of treatment. We find answers by funding research and we lead change by campaigning and collaborating.

In fact, whatever your particular concern in life, there are usually plenty of charities which will be happy to take a donation to support their efforts to deal with the issue that troubles you.

If breast cancer is your thing, you could donate your hard-earned cash to the £16.3 million-a-year Breakthrough Breast Cancer, or the £13.4 million-a-year Breast Cancer Care, or the £10.6 million-a-year a year Breast Cancer Campaign, or the £3.1 million-a-year Cancer Research Foundation, or the £2.4 million-a-year Breast Cancer Haven, or the £950,000 a year Against Breast Cancer Ltd., or the £629,000 a year Genesis Breast Cancer Prevention or the £182,000 a year Boot Out Breast Cancer or many other smaller charities all operating in this area.

Or perhaps the idea of the British population becoming unhealthily fat keeps you awake at night? Don't worry. There are plenty of charities that share your concerns. In Britain there are the Association for the Study of Obesity, HOOP (Help Overcoming Obesity Problems), the British Obesity

Society, Combating Obesity, Experts in Severe and Complex Obesity, Obesity Action Forum, Obesity Management Association and the Obesity Forum. In addition we have the European Association for the Study of Obesity and the World Obesity Federation.

A similar exercise could be carried out for most fields where there are numerous charities operating and it would probably show many charities in similar areas all seemingly doing strikingly similar work.

If there is duplication, triplication, quadruplication and worse amongst Britain's thousands upon thousands of charities, then this is probably costing ordinary members of the public who donate money and taxpayers, whose money the Government generously hands over to many of our charities, surprisingly large amounts of our cash. For example, if we just consider charities in England and Wales where there are reliable available figures, all charities with an income of £25,000 and above have to file independently-audited financial accounts with the Charity Commission. Assuming it costs an average of just £2,000 for accountants to audit a set of accounts for the 20,000 or so charities earning between £25,000 and £100,000, say £5,000 each in auditors' fees for the 20,871 charities collecting between £100,000 and £500,000, perhaps £7,000 each for the 8,302 charities picking up between £500,000 and £5 million and £25,000 each for the 1,976 big charities with over £5 million a year, then that's £252 million of donors' and taxpayers' money being used each year just for accountancy firms 'bean-counting' how much money the charities collect and spend.

Many charities try to get us to sign up to donating a small sum, maybe £5 or £10 a month. Just to pay the external auditors' fees for the 51,149 charities taking in £25,000 or more a year would require about four million people donating £5 per month or two million generous souls handing over a more substantial £10 per month.

Then there's the cost of the charities' executives and senior managers. For the moment, I'll just do a quick 'back of a fag packet' calculation only for those 10,278 charities in England and Wales which raise and spend over £500,000 a year. There is more detail on charity executives' and managers' salaries in Chapter 3 – *You Pay Peanuts*.

Assuming the 8,302 charities on £500,000 to £5,000,000 pay their management teams about £180,000 a year in total (in many cases it will be much more) and the 1,976 charities raising £5,000,000 or more a year pay their management £400,000 a year (some of the larger charities pay two to three times that), then there's a minimum of £2.3 billion of donors' and taxpayers' money going into the bank accounts of charity bosses and managers – the equivalent of 38 million people contributing £5 per month or 19 million giving £10 per month. And this £2.3 billion doesn't include the full-time and part-time management costs for the 144,358 charities in England and Wales earning less than £500,000 a year. Nor does it include the executives' and managers' costs for any of the 23,774 charities in Scotland or the 7,000 to 12,000 charities in Northern Ireland. In fact, if every working adult and every pensioner in Britain were to contribute £10 per month to charity, then the money raised probably wouldn't be enough to pay the salaries of just the executives and managers of our more than 195,289 registered charities.

Quote: *About ten years ago I flew to Bangkok and treated myself to Business Class. The gentleman sitting next to me was in his early thirties and when we got talking, it turns out that he ran a Nepalese children's charity. He was on his way to Kathmandu and flew that same trip four to five times a year. He opened his wallet to give me his card and there were more gold credit cards than I could shake a stick at. He told me that his job was very fulfilling. When I returned to the UK, I googled children's Nepalese charities and it turned out that his was just one of about ten that existed at that time*

Moreover, if we assume that all the 10,278 charities in England and Wales raising over £500,000 a year (plus the larger charities in Scotland and Northern Ireland) have offices, computers, printers, smartphones and all the other paraphernalia of modern organisational life, then truly enormous amounts of donors' and taxpayers' money are being swallowed up by these more than 10,278 larger charities' internal administration.

Time to slim down?

Some people are beginning to understand that there may be too many charities all doing similar things, all campaigning to raise our awareness about similar issues and all seeking our financial support for their particular hobby-horse. In fact, the three prostate cancer charities featured in Figure 2 – the Prostate

Cancer Research Foundation, Prostate Action and Prostate Cancer UK – seem to have realised that there was some overlap in their work and laudably decided to merge into just one charity. In 2011 the Prostate Cancer Research Foundation merged with Prostate Action. Then in 2012 this merged charity joined the much larger Prostate Cancer UK. Even in its first year, this merger of these three charities appears to have given significant savings in management and support costs thus releasing more money for real charitable purposes and for funding research.

In the year before the merger - 2011-12 - Prostate Action spent £2,040,086. Of this £1,177,112 went on charitable activities and research grants and £862,974 was spent on fundraising, management and administration. So, only 58 per cent of the money spent went to charity or grants. In the same year, Prostate Cancer UK spent £10,450,000, of which £7,034,000 was used for charitable activities and research grants and £3,417,000 for support costs. Thus 67 per cent of its expenditure was used for charity.

But a year later, the merged charity spent £20,694,000 of which £16,559,000 was directed at charitable activities and research grants and £4,135,000 on internal running costs and fundraising. This merged charity was now able to use a much larger 80 per cent for charitable purposes and grants. Part of the reason the percentage going to charity and research rose so much was due to more money being spent and less being retained by the charity in 2012-13 (£8.7 million) than in 2011-12 (£12.9 million). But the rise in charitable spending as a percentage of all spending was also partly due to economies of scale - more being done with a lower overall level of management and support costs because of less duplication of effort.

We can see these economies of scale in several areas. Fundraising seems to have become much more cost effective. In the year before the merger, 2011-12, Prostate Action raised £2,138,000 million for a fundraising cost of £751,000. Over at Prostate Cancer UK £23,330,000 was raised for a cost of £3,269,000. So, together these two separate charities raised £25,468,000 for a cost of £4,020,000 - £6.33 raised for every pound spent. In 2012-13, the merged charity raised £29,377,000 for a cost of £4,135,000 – now £7.10 for every pound spent – a rise of 12 per cent in fundraising effectiveness.

In 2011-12 Prostate Cancer UK spent £15,000 on communication and Prostate Action an additional £21,600 – a total of £36,600. Yet in 2012-13 the merged charity only used £22,000 for communications. Similarly in audit fees, Prostate Cancer UK paid £12,000 in 2011-12 and Prostate Action £9,600 – a total of £21,600. Yet a year later the combined charity only paid £15,000 for its audit. And in governance costs, in 2012-12 the two separate charities paid £248,159, yet in 2012-13 for the merged charity this had fallen to £206,000 (see Figure 3)

Figure 3 – Combining similar charities can lead to falling administrative costs and more money available for charitable activities

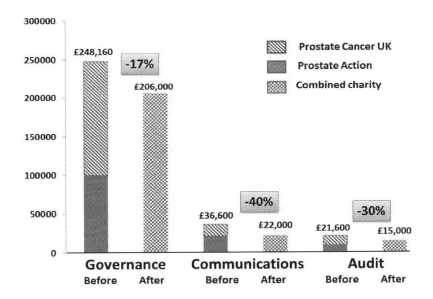

So, just in the first year, this merger seems to have reduced governance costs by 17 per cent, communications spending by 40 per cent and audit costs by 30 per cent.

The chief executive of one of the merging prostate cancer charities explained the reasons for their decision to combine forces, 'Merging increases efficiency. Previously, Prostate Cancer Research Foundation and Prostate UK were two very similar organisations. They often funded the same research projects, and even at one stage had trustees in common. Merging has streamlined us – we only need one office, one database, and can raise more money with our combined resources (including the trustees) and fund more work. Merging can aid fundraising: Merging has made us consider new forms of fundraising that we had not used before'.[4]

In 2009, two of Britain's largest charities supporting older people – Age Concern and Help the Aged merged to form Age UK. In the first year alone, this merger enabled the two charities to cut costs by around £8.4 million, including £5.2 million from staff reductions. This was the largest charity merger since Cancer Research Campaign and Imperial Cancer research joined forces in 2002 to form Cancer Research UK. But given the huge number of active registered charities in the UK and the similarities between many charities in some areas of work, the quantity of mergers could appear to be pitifully small.

Even the *Guardian*, that normally stalwart champion of ever more often unnecessary jobs (often called 'non-jobs') in the public and charity sectors, seems to have started wondering whether we really need so many charities. In a recent article, a writer asked, 'There are 163,000 charities, according to the Charity Commission, and thousands more voluntary organisations are recognised as charitable but are unregistered. Should there be so many?' The writer then went on to suggest the possibly previously blasphemous idea that charities should consider merging, 'Companies merge to make more profit, public sector bodies are reorganised to provide better services – maybe charities should do the same'. One can hardly imagine the gasps of horror from typical *Guardian* readers at the thought of public-sector employees or charity workers becoming more efficient.

The *Guardian* writer appeared to recognise that the main barrier to charity mergers may not be the desirability or practicality of the merger and the benefits the merger might produce for those the charities were founded to help, but rather the risk of the people involved wanting to protect their own jobs, territory and self-importance, 'Trustees must always ask whether a charity's objectives are best served by using resources themselves or passing them on to others who are better placed to help beneficiaries. If this question was objectively addressed by charity trustees, I believe there would be many more collaborations and full mergers between charities'.[5]

Perhaps even more astonishing than the *Guardian* printing this heretical article suggesting charity mergers was the fact that all the *Guardian* readers who commented on the article actually agreed. One wrote, 'Yes please. We are crying out for it in the environmental sector' and this was echoed by several others. Though one reader worried, *'Yes, but what would happen to all those extraneous (sic) Chief Executives with fat pay packets? It would mean the self-serving David Miliband types would have to come back into politics to feather their nests'*.

The Charity Commission also seems to support the idea of charities merging for the common good. On its website, the Commission provides advice on the process charities should use to merge because, as the Charity Commission explains, 'charities can merge into one organisation to be more efficient or share resources. You may want your charity to merge with another to make better use of charitable funds and property, and provide better services for your beneficiaries. For example if two charities in the same area are doing similar work and competing for funding, a merger may be the best way to secure funding and provide a united voice'.

Parkinson's Disease?

The number of active registered charities in England and Wales has remained relatively constant over the last fifteen years. There were 163,355 in 1999. This reached 169,297 just before the financial crash and then fell back again to 164,515 by 2014. But there has been a massive rise in the number of charities with annual income in excess of £10 million a year. This shot up from just 307 at the start of the 'Brown and Balls Boom' to 747 by the time of the 'Brown and Balls Bust' in 2008 and continued to rocket ever upwards to 1,005 by 2013 (see Figure 4)

Figure 4 – There has been a huge increase in the number of charities with income above £10 million a year

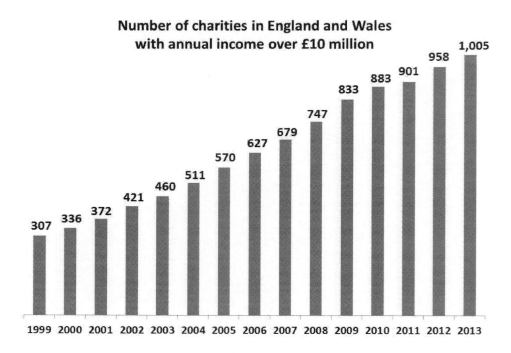

Number of charities in England and Wales with annual income over £10 million

1999	2000	2001	2002	2003	2004	2005	2006	2007	2008	2009	2010	2011	2012	2013
307	336	372	421	460	511	570	627	679	747	833	883	901	958	1,005

There are various possible explanations as to why the number of larger charities – those with income above £10 million a year - should have more than doubled from 307 to 747 during the boom and then gone up again by another 258 from 747 to 1,005 following the bust. A positive interpretation would be as follows – during the boom we all got richer and so could donate ever more money to charity, then during the bust we kept on generously donating to help all those people and animals and other things affected by the economic crash.

However, there is also an alternative, slightly less generous interpretation of the tripling in the number of charities with income of above £10 million a year in the fifteen years since 1999. Writing in the *Economist* in 1955 Cyril Northcote Parkinson gave us what came to be known as Parkinson's Law: *'Work expands so as to fill the time available for its completion'*. While employed in the British Civil Service, Parkinson observed that a bureaucracy will grow at a rate of five to seven per cent a year *'irrespective of any variation in the amount of work (if any) to be done'*. One example he gave was from the Royal Navy where, between 1914 and 1928, the number of ships fell by 68 per cent and the number of sailors by 32 per cent. At the same time, the number of dockyard managers went up by 40 per cent and the number of Admiralty officials increased by 78 per cent. Parkinson had identified and quantified what we now call 'scope creep' - how bureaucracies and professional organisations always seem to find increasing quantities of real or fictitious work for themselves which leads to the apparent necessity for them to keep growing, keep hiring more staff and as a result keep paying themselves ever more because of the increasing amount of work they either have to do or else enthusiastically create for themselves.

Figure 5 – There has been a decline in 'real jobs' in Britain but a massive increase in middlemen and administrators

We saw this phenomenon in the British private sector. In the thirty three years from 1980 to 2013, the number of solicitors in Britain rocketed up from about 37,800 to over 120,000; the number of accountants from around 100,000 to above 325,000 and estate agents from around 165,000 to more than 562,000.

At the same time, the number of those employed in construction was fairly stagnant and the number working in manufacturing halved (see Figure 5)

There was a similar situation in politics. In 1997, we had 650 MPs at Westminster. In spite of the fact that we keep reducing the power of the British Parliament by handing over ever more decision-making to the rapidly expanding and increasingly expensive Brussels bureaucracy, by 2014 we also had 129 Members of the Scottish Parliament, 108 Members of the Legislative Assembly of Northern Ireland and 60 Members of the Welsh Assembly in addition to our 650 Westminster MPs. In fact, we had so many politicians in Britain doing ever less law-making, that the Westminster Parliament started shortening its sessions and increasing MPs' holidays each year as they ran out of anything useful to do. Moreover, in 2012 MPs were awarded a large increase in the amount of money they could use to pay for more staff to help them do ever less work. This went up by twenty per cent from £115,000 a year to £137,200 a year for non-London MPs and to £144,000 for those with constituencies inside the capital.

We can also see Parkinson's principle of how bureaucracies grow occurring throughout our public sector. Though the figures suggest that growth in British bureaucracy first under New Labour and then the Coalition has been much faster than even Parkinson predicted, in spite of successive governments' assurances about efficiency and belt-tightening and bonfires of quangos. The budget for the Financial Services Authority, the regulator for the financial services industry, for example spiralled impressively upwards from £29 million in 1997 to over £526 million a year by 2013, the year in which it was scrapped for being ineffective in spite of the vast amounts of our money it was effortlessly consuming. In 2006-7, the year before the financial crisis, the budget for Ofwat, the regulator for the water industry that has done so embarrassingly little to control the water companies' increasing charges and profits, was £11.5 million. By 2012-13, in spite of the crisis and the Government's much vaunted and much criticised austerity, Ofwat's budget had reached £20.1 million and then rose again in the following year to £27.9 million – more than doubling in just seven years. Something similar seems to have been happening over at Ofgem, the regulator for the gas and electricity markets which has impotently allowed our electricity bills to rocket ever upwards. Ofgem's costs leapt up from £38.8 million in 2006-7 to £73.3 million by 2012-13 and then to £83.3 million by 2013-14.

In our supposedly 'cash-strapped' NHS, in 1997 when New Labour first came to power, there were about 200,000 hospital beds and 25,000 managers - around eight beds per manager. Yet by 2014 we had just under 140,000 hospital beds and about 38,000 managers – less than four beds per manager. Of course, the number of hospital beds is not by any means a comprehensive indicator of NHS activity, especially as some conditions which previously required hospitalisation can now be treated by day clinics. However, the fact that the number of hospital beds fell by 30 per cent while the number of managers rose by 52 per cent does suggest that the NHS may be suffering from the same kind of 'Parkinsonian' managerialisation and bureaucratisation that we have seen throughout the British public sector (see Figure 6)

Figure 6 – The public sector seems to do ever less with ever more people

(% change from 1997 to 2014)

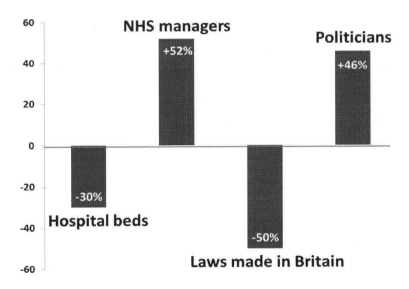

One commentator coined the expression 'spurious activity' to describe this situation where the bureaucrats and vested interest groups like lawyers and accountants continually find reasons to expand their empires, often at huge and unnecessary cost to society.[6]

Many of our larger charities seem to have been successful in impressive scope creep - expanding their workload by finding new and important issues to put on their agenda. For example, in addition to its main mission of tackling the 'causes and consequences of poverty', Christian Aid has started campaigning against supposed Man-Made Global Warming and against tax avoidance. Also, both Christian Aid and CAFOD have worked to stop the building of a new airport in the Thames estuary – the so-called 'Boris Island'.

War on Want's main mission is to fight 'poverty in developing countries in partnership and solidarity with people affected by globalisation'. Yet War on Want's many campaigns have reportedly included 'fighting supermarket power, abolishing the World Trade Organisation, boycotting Israeli goods, "Justice for Palestine", occupying Waitrose and "working closely with trade unions, UK Uncut, and the Tax Justice Network to highlight the devastating impact of swingeing cuts to public services"'.[7]

The National Council for Marriage Guidance was founded in 1938 by a clergyman Dr Herbert Grey to provide a counselling service for husbands and wives. In 1988, it changed its name to Relate after it had broadened its service to include unmarried couples and same-sex couples in addition to its original target – married couples. Moreover, the range of services Relate was offering also seemed to expand impressively, 'Relate delivers via a national network a wide range of services to individuals and corporate bodies. Activities include: relationship counselling, sex therapy, family counselling, services for young people, mediation services, counselling in primary care settings, telephone counselling, online relationship assessment service, national email counselling service, education and learning, etc'.[8]

Relate, which is largely funded by taxpayers, also gets involved in child poverty, anti-social behaviour, flexible working hours and legal rights for unmarried couples and now claims it is 'delivering inclusive, high-quality services that are relevant at every stage of life'.[9] Similarly, in 2012 the School Food Trust cleverly changed its name to 'the Children's Food Trust' thus giving itself huge amounts of extra work campaigning for better food children in their 'early years' as well as for those at school.

And the much loved Royal National Lifeboat Institution has branched out into spending £11.1 million a year of donors' money providing Baywatch-style, strikingly-dressed, athletic young lifeguards at more than two hundred, largely safe British beaches during the summer – at a cost of around £50,000 of donors' money per beach per summer season.

These are just a few examples of the way our larger charities can become ever larger through effective use of scope creep. A quick look at the activities and claimed successes of many of our better-known charities will usually show them getting involved in an often impressive plethora of campaigns and political issues and other efforts that are not obviously, clearly and closely related to the causes for which they were originally founded and for which we give them our money.

Quote: *I spent several years as a volunteer with a major charity. During that time I noted the growing influence of professional charity managers who seemed to conspire at changing, re-formatting, re-launching and generally keeping everything in a state of flux so that their time was filled and their jobs justified. Money raised from the public, that had once been mostly spent on providing the charity's front-line service, was increasingly spent on the hire of hotels for weekend sessions spent briefing new policies and new procedures to the volunteers. Travelling instructors were paid to visit all our centres of operation and give lessons on the new methods. Meanwhile, professional policy-makers at the HQ schemed how the charity's remit was to be extended into new areas.*[10]

Chapter 2

What is charity?

The Charity Commission for England and Wales claims that £53 billion of the £63 billion raised is spent on what it calls 'charitable activities'. That's a quite impressive £8.41 of every £10 raised. The *Oxford English Dictionary* defines charity as 'the voluntary giving of help, typically in the form of money, to those in need'. But the definition of 'charitable activities' used by the Charity Commission and charities might seem rather relaxingly broad to many people from outside the charity industry. In fact, a closer look at the accounts of some of Britain's charities could suggest that the amount actually going towards real 'charitable activities' as defined in our best-known dictionary may be less than £5 for every £10 donated – rather far below the £8.41 asserted by the Charity Commission.

If we just take two of Britain's best-loved and largest charities (which shall remain nameless) and have a quick shifty through their annual reports, then we can get a better feel for where our money really ends up.

Like many charities, Charity A generates some of its income from 'commercial activities' (selling stuff). In the latest financial year, £21 million of the £122 million this charity raised came from these commercial activities. The costs of its commercial activities appear to be £18.4 million. So, of the £21 million raised by selling things, only £2.6 million actually seems to have gone into the central kitty to be used for charitable purposes, management and administration. Thus out of every £10 taken by its shops, just £1.24 was left to be used for charitable purposes and administration. The other £8.76 was spent getting things for the shops and running the shops. This might worry some people who may have thought that a goodly proportion of the money they spent in this charity's shops was going to good causes.

Of the £122 which Charity A raised, it spent £115 million and retained £7 million for future use. The £115 million can be split into £32.5 million generating its income and £82.6 million on what it classed as 'charitable spending'. So, only about £7.18 of every £10 spent could have been used for charitable purposes. Although this is a fair bit below the £8.41 the Charity Commission claims is the average spent on charitable activities for all charities in England and Wales, this would probably be quite acceptable to most of those who had donated the £115 million this charity used. But we need to examine what this charity has included in the £82.6 million it classed as 'charitable expenditure'.

This charity has many thousands of members and spent £4 million managing its membership which raised £32 million. Some people might be tempted to see this £4 million as 'administration' rather than genuine charitable expenditure. But Charity A decided to include the £4 million under 'charitable expenditure' in its accounts and this seems to have been either not noticed or accepted by its auditors and by the Charity Commission. Another £14.2 million of the £82.6 million 'charitable expenditure' was used for what the charity described as 'Education and Communication' – some of this could also be seen as political campaigning, something that has recently attracted quite a lot of criticism from outside the charity industry (see Chapter 5 – *Playing Politics*).

Figure 1 – It's not obvious how much of Charity A's spending went into real charitable activities

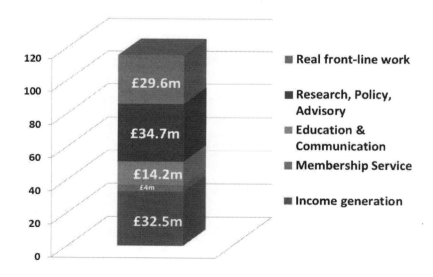

Another £34.7 million went on 'Research, Policy and Advisory'. We don't know what this includes, so it's difficult to judge whether this would fit into what donors would consider as genuine 'charitable expenditure'. And the final £29.6 million – just £2.57 of every £10 spent - was actually used for the proper front-line work that many donors might normally associate with this charity (see Figure 1)

Charity B is also a stalwart of the charity industry. On the charity's website, a spokesperson for Charity B claimed that the charity spends £8.40 of every £10 raised 'saving lives'. So that's pretty close to the Charity Commission's average of £8.41.

Charity B seems to have three main sources of funds – shops, public donations and government grants. Its shops raised £89.9 million of its total income of £385.5 million, but cost £67.6 million to run, leaving just £22.3 million for charity. So, just £2.48 out of every £10 spent in Charity B's shops actually goes into its central coffers to be used for saving lives, administration, campaigning, fundraising and management. The other £7.52 is spent running the shops, in spite of the fact that the people working in the shops are mostly volunteers, most of what they sell is donated, the charity pays either hugely reduced or no business rates and it may be getting some of its premises rent-free as freeholders, anxious to avoid paying full business rates on empty properties, often allow charities to use them for either a nominal sum or else free of charge as charity shops are mostly exempt from business rates.

In addition to its commercial activities, Charity B raises about £295.6 million in donations with a cost for raising this money of £23 million. So it appears to get an impressive £13 in for every £1 used to raise money. However, £159.8 million of these donations come from government, large taxpayer-funded institutions and public authorities. So, actually about £135.8 million is raised from us directly at a cost of £23 million. But that's still a very respectable £6 raised for every £1 spent on fundraising.

Now we know that of the £385.5 million raised by Charity B from its shops, public donations and government grants, £90.6 million of this is spent getting the money in - £67.6 million running the shops plus £23 million for other fundraising activities. That leaves about £294.9 million - £7.65 for every £10 raised - to be spent 'saving lives'. That's already a little bit less than the spokesperson's claim of £8.40 of every £10 being used for 'saving lives'.

Then we have to knock off about £31.9 million for support and governance costs, leaving £263 million – 68 per cent of the £385.5 million raised – available for charity work. Now, at just £6.82 for every £10 raised we're even further below the charity's claim of £8.40 of every £10 spent 'saving lives'.

But of the £263 million supposedly available for charitable work, about 34 per cent (£90.6 million) isn't spent directly by Charity B on its own projects. Instead, this £90.6 million is handed out in grants to other charities. As these other charities receiving grants from Charity B will certainly have their own managerial and administrative costs of twenty per cent or more, there's at least another £18.1 million not available for real charity. That leaves us with £244.9 million – 63.5 per cent of the £385.5 million raised by Charity B for 'saving lives' (see Figure 2)

Figure 2 – How much of Charity B's money is really used for 'saving lives'?

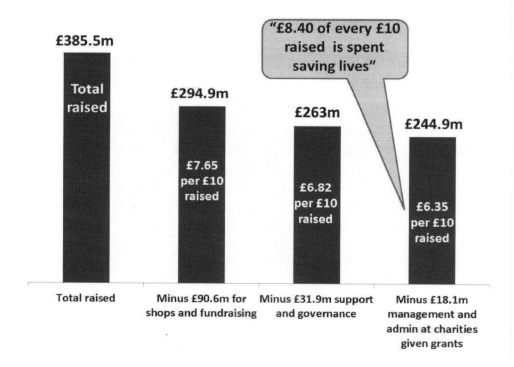

So, on these calculations, only about £6.35 of every £10 raised by Charity B really can go to 'saving lives'. This is considerably lower than the £8.40 the charity quotes when trying to attract our money by reassuring us most of our money will be spent 'saving lives'. Moreover, Charity B spends £21.7 million on 'Campaigning and Advocacy'. These are probably useful and enjoyable activities. But they may not be what the average member of the public thinks of when they hear the words 'saving lives'. So, we're now down to just £5.79 of every £10 raised that could be spend on 'saving lives'.

Then there's one other not inconsiderable problem. Charity B operates extensively throughout the Third World and many experts, audits and UN special studies suggest that a significant amount – between a third and two thirds depending on the recipient country - of the aid given to many Third World countries disappears due to corruption and mismanagement (see Chapter 6 – *The Foreign Aid Farrago*). So, it's quite possible, or even probable, that less than half the money given to Charity B is actually effectively used for 'saving lives'. That's likely to be a lot less than people donating money would have expected and certainly an awful lot less than the £8.40 the spokesperson claimed.

We can face similar problems identifying how much of our money is really used for genuine charitable purposes in many smaller charities. Charity C, for example, spent only £137,673 of the £235,609 raised in 2012 on 'charitable activities'. That's just 58 per cent of its income. A year later in 2013 it used £140,974 on 'charitable activities' out of £296,975 raised – only 47 per cent of its income. However, within 'charitable activities' were things like 'admin support' - £23,182 in 2012 and £25,155 in 2013 and 'fundraising expenses' - £9,163 in 2012 and £8,906 in 2013. These fundraising expenses included under 'charitable activities' were in addition to the £85,000 paid in 2012 and £155,020 used in 2013 as 'costs of generating funds'. The 'charitable activities' also included 'travel' £9,737 in 2012 and £7,172 in 2013 and 'rent' paid to the founder - £6,000 in each year (see Figure 3).

**Figure 3 – How much of Charity C's 2013 income was spent on
what most people would consider 'charitable activities'?**

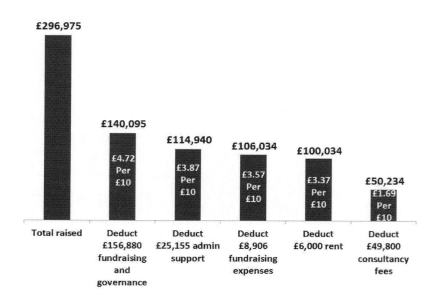

Many other charities class items such as admin support, rent and fundraising expenses as running costs rather than, as in this case, 'charitable activities'. Moreover in 2012, the charity's founder was paid £47,186 in 'consultancy fees' and another £49,800 'consultancy fees' in 2013. The charity classed these consultancy fees as 'charitable activities' and they accounted for 34 per cent of charitable spending in 2012 and 35 per cent of charitable spending in 2013. Now, some people will feel it is right that someone putting the effort into setting up a charity should be rewarded for their time and contribution. Moreover, there may even be people who believe these consultancy fees should be permitted to be classed as 'charitable activities' by both the auditors and the Charity Commission. However, there may be others who would feel a sense of unease if they knew just how much of the donated money was paid out to this charity's founder each year in consultancy fees under the heading 'charitable activities'.

A rigorous examination of Charity C's accounts might conclude that only about £1.69 of every £10 raised was really being used for genuine charitable activities. In fact, given that the founder was handed £49,800 in consultancy fees from the charity while the charity used at most £50,234 for charitable activities, there may even be questions about whether Charity C should even have charitable status at all.

A 2013 parliamentary enquiry into the charity sector found there were so many charities that the Charity Commission for England and Wales was struggling just to ensure that most registered charities were really genuine charities rather than tax avoidance schemes or political campaigning groups masquerading as charities. The enquiry judged that the Commission, which was receiving over nine hundred calls, letters and emails every single working day, didn't have the staff to check whether the tens of billions of pounds, which our more than a hundred thousand charities claimed to be using for 'charitable activities', were actually going to real charitable purposes at all. So the enquiry concluded that the Charity Commission had not been and would never be successful in promoting 'the effective use of charitable resources'.[11].

Chapter 3

You Pay Peanuts

Noise and fury

From time to time, there's an eruption of press outrage as charity bosses are accused of being greedy and over-paid. Then we get angry headlines such as *'Nine British charities paid staff over £300k each last year'* and *'Charity chief's £653,000 pay reignites row'* and *'Save the Children executives shared £160,000 bonus pot'* and *'Ministers refuse to punish charities that pay staff over £100k a year'*. These accusations of charity bosses being 'fat-cats' allegedly living in luxury paid for with donors' money play out particularly well with the public at a time of austerity when ordinary people see their earnings frozen while prices of essentials such as food, housing, fuel and power rise ever upwards at a much faster rate than the official inflation figures suggest.

So, when such articles appear, there are always a few MPs readily available to express our outrage and conveniently get their names in the mainstream media for apparently championing ordinary people's interests, while busily increasing their own salaries and expenses. Politicians have recently announced, 'these figures are staggering. It is clear that in parts of the charity sector, some charities' pay is excessive'. There was also, 'there are real questions whether trustees are acting responsibly in approving pay packages that would seem to be out of control to the person in the street'. And we were treated to, 'the Charity Commission must step in and look at the charitable tax status of these organisations'. Meanwhile, an article in the Guardian predictably fought back with a slightly less than original headline, *'If you pay charity bosses peanuts, you'll get monkeys'*.[12] Although, after a few days of highly animated heat and noise but little light, the furore usually dies down, something else occupies newspaper headline writers and everything continues as before.

Faced with such accusations of 'fat-cattery', charity bosses are quick to defend themselves. So we're told how complicated it is to run a major charity,

'The big national and international charities are very demanding jobs and we need to attract the best talent to those jobs and that's what we do'. Or charities claim that donors want them to employ the best people, 'This simply isn't an issue for donors. They are more concerned about the outcomes, the performance and the efficiency of these organisations'. Or else charity bosses appeal to our consciences, 'I suspect the public do understand that this is means and ends: the end is getting aid to people who desperately need it'.

Mine's smaller than yours

One of the reasons charities give to justify the salaries of their bosses is to claim that they are reasonable compared to salaries for running comparable organisations in the private and public sectors. So, it might be worth taking a moment to look at what has been happening to executive and managerial pay in these other areas in order to judge whether charity bosses' salaries are acceptable or excessive.

Executhieves strike gold

The last few years may have been a little tough for many of us. But for the captains of Britain's largest companies they've been a time of glorious largesse and generosity to themselves. In the fifteen years between 1999 and 2014, the value of Britain's top one hundred companies – the FTSE100 – has dropped by over a third in real terms after taking account of inflation. However, this unfortunate and impressively massive destruction of the value of the companies they ran doesn't seem to have affected the pay packets of these companies' bosses. In fact, the rewards for failure have been remarkable. In 1999, the average remuneration package of FTSE100 executives was just over £1 million – including salary, pension contributions and various incentive schemes. By 2014, the average CEO remuneration package had topped £4.1 million – equivalent to about £3 million after taking account of inflation. Perhaps seldom in British business history has such poor performance by so many been so well rewarded.

Public service or self service?

We can also see many similar examples of this kind of pay inflation in the public sector. Over the last ten years, the remuneration of the chief executive of Ofgem has gone up by 48 per cent, by around 76 per cent at the BBC (though this fell back after public outcry and the departure of the £800,000+ a year Mark Thompson), by about around 99 per cent at Ofcom and by 126 per cent at the Bank of England.

Perhaps the worst examples of public-sector pay inflation are in our local councils – the ones that claim they have to cut services due to a lack of money. In 2007, just before the financial collapse and the recession, there were in the region of 600 people in local councils being paid £100,000 a year or more, 64 on £150,000 a year or more, 5 on £200,000 a year or above and none earning anything near £250,000. Yet by 2013, after years of supposed 'we're all in this together' austerity, there were a more impressive 2,181 on £100,000 or more, 542 on £150,000 a year or more and 34 on £250,000 a year or above (see Figure 1)

Figure 1 – We have been very generous to council executives and managers

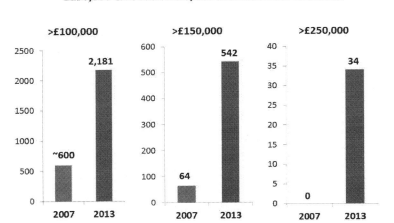

Number of council staff paid more than £100,000, than £150,000 and than £250,000 between 2007 and 2013

Over the same period, the average remuneration package of the ten highest-paid council executives jumped from about £203,000 a year to above £270,000 a year – a rise of 33 per cent during one of the worst recessions in British history.

The 'charity discount'

Compared to what has been happening at the top levels of business and the public sector, pay for charity executives can seem quite modest. Just over ninety per cent of registered charities have no paid staff and fewer than one per cent of charities have any employees earning £60,000 or more a year. Moreover, charity salaries seem to be lower than the private and public sectors with about 1.2 per cent of paid charity staff getting £60,000 or more a year compared to 4.5 per cent in the public sector and over 6 per cent in the private sector.

Charity bosses used to be paid less than people in similar positions in both the public and private sectors. But the most recent research suggests that in the last fifteen years salaries for charity executives and managers have caught up with those in the public sector, but are still considerably below those in the private sector. This has led to what some people call the 'charity discount' – people working for charities accept being paid less than those in equivalent jobs in the private sector because of the personal satisfaction of doing charity work. A recent report estimated the 'charity discount' compared to private-sector salaries to be somewhere between 25 and 45 per cent.[13]

However charity bosses, especially those at the larger charities, can expect other benefits which private-sector executives are unlikely to get. There's the social cachet of charity work and the top dogs at the major charities may get gongs or even a seat in the Lords as a reward for their supposed 'sacrifices'. In addition, thanks to their public image as great altruists selflessly helping the needy, they will often land lucrative jobs as either real contributors to, or possibly just impressive figureheads on, the boards of many other public- and private-sector organisations.

Poverty for some

But even though they are paid far less than their private-sector counterparts, our charity chiefs are far from living in penury. For those in the best-paying charities, there does seem to be a reasonable amount of money sloshing around. The most recent estimates are that around 16,000 charity staff are paid more than £60,000 a year and of these perhaps 3,000 are getting over £100,000 a year. Moreover in recent few years, we may be seeing similar salary inflation in charity bosses' pay to that which we've had in companies and government departments, defying the austerity and pay freezes many ordinary people have experienced since the 2008 financial crash.

If we just look at a few of the largest charities dealing with poverty, we can see that their bosses don't seem to be suffering quite as much as the people they serve:

Oxfam - The £368 million-a-year, 5,046-employee Oxfam appears to be one of the more frugal of the largest poverty charities in the matter of executive remuneration. Between the start of the recession in 2008 and the end of 2013, the chief executive's pay only rose by about 7 per cent from £101,754 to £108,575 – well below inflation

Save the Children - Things look a bit brighter for the leader at the £284 million-a-year, 4,025-employee Save the Children. Here the highest-paid person's remuneration rose from £128,310 in 2008 to £168,653 in 2012 (at the time of writing the 2013 figure was not available) – a rise of 31 per cent

Red Cross Society - At the £228 million-a-year, 3,200-employee Red Cross Society (UK) the highest-paid person's remuneration rose from somewhere between £170,000-£180,000 to somewhere between £200,000-£210,000 – an increase of about 18 per cent

Christian Aid - At the rather smaller £95 million-a-year, 854-employee Christian Aid, there appears to have been a fairly substantial pay rise too. The highest paid employee's salary rose by 40 per cent from £90,123 in 2008 to £126,206 in 2013 (though the 2013 salary was for a different person). Curiously, the top earner at the £95 million-a-year, 854-employee Christian Aid, received £17,631 more than the chief executive of the much larger £368 million-a-year, 5,046-employee Oxfam. Christian Aid has, of course, defended its boss's pay package, 'we want to reassure you that we make every effort to avoid paying higher salaries than are necessary. We pay our staff salaries the same as, or below, the median of other church-based and/or international development agencies'[14]

ActionAid - At the £59 million-a-year, 145-employee ActionAid, the highest paid executive's salary only rose by 12 per cent between 2008 and 2012 from £79,265 to £88,933 (2013's figures were not available at the time of writing)

Cafod - At the £49 million-a-year, 444-employee Cafod, the highest paid employee's salary rose by 27 per cent from £71,258 to £90,464 – comfortably above inflation (see Figure 2).

Figure 2 – Some anti-poverty charities have possibly been generous with their highest paid employees in the recession years of 2008 to 2013

(Rise in pay for the highest paid employee)

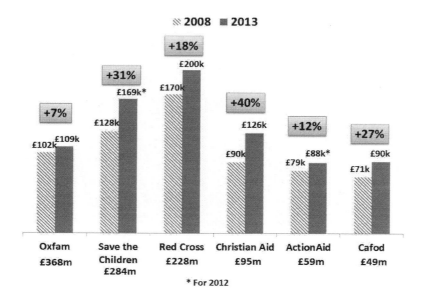

Executive salaries at some of these anti-poverty charities may have increased considerably over the last few years. But in spite of this, apart from perhaps at Christian Aid, there isn't really any compelling evidence of excessive pay given the size and complexity of some of these organisations. Where the real pay problem might be is that there are so many, no doubt worthy, organisations all doing pretty much the same thing for the same people in the same countries. That then poses the question – why do we need so many anti-poverty charities all with their chief executives and fundraising managers and financial directors and commercial directors and so on?

Just these six anti-poverty charities have 142 executives and managers being paid £60,000 a year or more and of these there are seventeen with salaries of £100,000 or more (see Figure 3)

Figure 3 – The number of executives and managers at each salary level for the largest six anti-poverty and emergency aid charities

	Oxfam	Save the Children	Red Cross	Christian Aid	ActionAid	Cafod
Income	£368m	£284m	£228m	£95.4m	£59.4m	£48.8m
£60k-£70k	17	16	19	8	5	3
£70k-£80k	13	8	1	-	2	2
£80k-£90k	6	5	6	4	1	-
£90k-£100k	4	1	3	-	-	-
£100k-£110k	2	2	2	-	-	-
£110k-£120k	1	5	2	-	-	-
£120k-£130k	-	-	1	1	-	-
£130k-£140k	-	-	-	-	-	-
£140k-£150k	-	-	-	-	-	-
£150k-£160k	-	-	-	-	-	-
£160k +	-	-	1 (£205k+)	-	-	-
Total	**43**	**38**	**35**	**13**	**8**	**5**

The lottery winners

While there don't seem to be too many indications of hugely excessive pay at the larger, best-known charities, the rewards dished out at some smaller charities could appear surprisingly magnanimous. There are so many charities that the potential 'over-payers' can be difficult to find. However, here are a few where one might wonder at the level of the top dog's remuneration:

The Princess Diana Memorial Trust has now ceased operation. But in its heyday, it was distributing about £6.3 million a year. At that time it had one executive on £110,000 to £120,000 a year. This person was only managing 15 staff. The chief executive of Oxfam is paid slightly less (£108,775) and is responsible for over five thousand staff

The Serpentine Trust manages two quite small art galleries in Central London. The original gallery – the Serpentine Gallery - is housed in a modestly-sized former tea pavilion built in 1934. In 2013 the Serpentine Sackler Gallery was opened to the public, giving new life to The Magazine, a former gunpowder store built in 1805. Located five minutes' walk from the Serpentine Gallery across the Serpentine Bridge, it comprises 900 square metres of gallery space. The Serpentine Trust's income in 2013 was just over £6.7 million and it paid its chief executive somewhere between £110,000 and £120,000. This chief executive, also paid more than the boss of the 5,046-person Oxfam, was responsible for 57 staff

Keep Britain Tidy had income in 2013 of £7.8 million and paid its chief executive between £90,000 and £100,000 to look after the activities of its 122 employees.

Given that none of the three charities mentioned above is operating internationally, none is working in war zones and all have quite small workforces, it might seem strange that their chief executives are all paid at around the same level as the head of Oxfam and more than the bosses of Cafod and ActionAid.

Chapter 4

Fundraising fun

Are you 'fun, inspiring and passionate'? Are you a 'driven individual with a FIRE in your belly'? Are you 'motivated and ethically minded'? Do you see yourself as 'a team player with a confident manner and a professional, flexible, positive and studious approach to your work'? Do you want to 'spend your days soaking up the glorious sunshine, meeting amazing new people and raising loads of money for charity'? Well then, what are you waiting for? Why don't you become a charity fundraiser?

Charities have many ways of raising money – TV ads, press ads, direct mailings, box-rattling collectors and so on. But the one that seems to have attracted the most media attention recently has been what the charities call 'Face to Face' fundraising, often abbreviated to 'F2F' fundraising. There have been several TV documentary and press exposés of the allegedly aggressive tactics of F2F street charity collectors, often stigmatised as 'charity muggers', usually shortened to 'chuggers'.

The *Oxford English Dictionary* definition of chugger is, 'A person who approaches passers-by in the street asking for subscriptions or donations to a particular charity' and the example of using the word the dictionary gives is *'When you have chuggers outside your shop, people just cross the road'*. The *Urban Dictionary* is even less complimentary about chuggers, 'Paid "charity" street worker who has been trained to believe that they are carrying out a worthy task, improving peoples' lives by conning Joe Public out of their money for this week's Good Cause. Usually an agency worker where the agency takes a hefty cut of the hourly rate that the charity in question has paid for, whilst at the same time increasing profits by selling on details of those foolish enough to actually stop and sign up to said Good Cause'. The *Urban Dictionary* then advises, *'If you really want to support a charity, do it through their website, not a chugger'*.

According to the regulator for chuggers – the Public Fundraising Regulatory Authority (PFRA) - F2F fundraising was first used by Greenpeace in Austria in 1995, 'On one particularly hot summer day in 1995 in northern Austria, one team of fundraisers found repeatedly that no-one was answering the door. They realised that everyone was out enjoying the nice weather and so the fundraisers decided to relocate themselves to the local swimming pool to find the people who were not at home. And so a new fundraising technique was born'. Greenpeace quickly adopted chugging in other countries and launched its first British chugging campaign in 1997. Seeing Greenpeace's success with chugging, many other British charities also started using the technique and sometimes it seems you can't walk down your local high street or through your favourite shopping centre without being chugged, often several times, by different charities.

Box-rattlers are allowed to collect money. But chuggers aren't permitted to take cash directly from us. Instead they usually try to get us to set up a direct debit giving say £5 or £10 a month or else persuade us to send a text donating a few pounds. Most chuggers work for chugging agencies, not directly for the charities they may claim to represent, and chuggers are typically paid between £7.50 and £9.50 an hour depending on their level of experience.

With the cost of the chugger, their material and the chugger agencies' fees, charities will usually pay between £80 and £120 for each person who agrees to set up a direct debit. This means that pretty much all of a direct-debit donor's first year's donations and sometimes almost two years' donations will go into the bank accounts of the chugging agency and the chugger. It's only after this time that the charity gets any money at all. As for someone texting say £5 – that will pay for just a few minutes of chugger's time given the high fees the charity pays to the chugging agency. Perhaps that's why the *Urban Dictionary* sensibly advises us to donate through charity websites, not chuggers.

Research suggests that about half the people chugged cancel their direct debit within three months. Sometimes this can mean the charity actually loses money as it may have paid the agency the £80 to £120 for the donor's direct debit sign-up but will only have collected a couple of months' donations. However, the half that don't cancel have been found to keep their monthly donations going for an average of three to five years – and that's where the charity gets its money. Many charities claim that F2F fundraising is the most cost-effective way of raising money and ensuring longer-term donations and that, having a loyal core of donors giving a known amount each month, helps them plan their activities. Moreover, charities say chugging enables them to get the attention of young people who may be difficult to reach using more traditional fundraising methods. The usual return on F2F fundraising seems to be about 4:1 - £4 raised for every £1 spent on chugging.

Critics of chuggers have accused them of using excessive emotional pressure and even bullying and lies to get people to donate. But every time there's a TV or press investigation, the charities and chugging agencies involved always throw up their hands in amazement and horror while claiming they never imagined their fundraisers were being anything but honest, open and ethical (see Figure 1)

Figure 1 – Charities are quick to express surprise and concern when their fundraisers are caught breaking fundraising rules and even the law

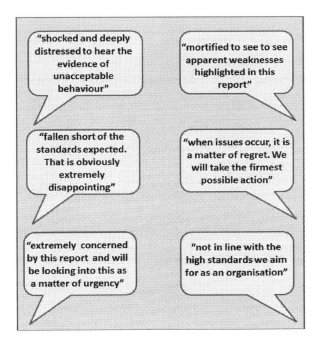

But a professor of voluntary sector management seemed less than convinced by the charities' and chugging agencies' professions of shocked innocence, 'it's inconceivable that a director of fundraising or the fundraiser responsible in the charity can't have some understanding of what's going on in an agency with which they have a contract'.[15] There have now been so many exposés of aggressive chugging, all of which reveal the same problems, that a cynic might imagine the charities' and chugging agencies' PR departments already have their pre-printed 'we were astonished and horrified' and 'not up to our usual high standards' and 'we will take immediate action' statements ready to be sent out at the slightest whiff of trouble.

We don't pay commission

When accused of harassing members of the public to extract money from us, one of the main defences used by charities and chugging agencies is that their staff are salaried and are not paid commissions. So their people are supposedly under absolutely no financial pressure to sign up direct-debit donors or texters. One charity – a major user of chugging – claimed 'fundraisers are not given personal financial targets'. Many members of the public seem to believe the 'no-commission' story – 'the bottom line is that face-to-face fundraisers work really hard, get abused mentally and physically and keep smiling for £9 per hour....They do not get commission and they raise millions of pounds a year to help homeless people, people with cancer, children, the list is endless'.[16] However, in an article explaining the tactics he used to get people to sign up, one chugger explained, 'there are tough targets, and penalties for missing them. The staff turnover rate among fundraisers makes the job of Chelsea manager look ironclad'.[17] Moreover, a failed chugger admitted, 'I worked as a chugger but only lasted one week. My agency paid commission and the targets were tough. Seeing how pushy some of my colleagues were made me quit. I was quite uneasy, especially as if you earned over a certain amount you got 40 per cent – think how little the charity would get after the agency took its fee'.[18]

Though they say they don't pay commission, almost all chugging agencies seem to pay what they call 'bonuses'. When you look at the job ads for street charity fundraisers, it's very difficult to find one that doesn't offer bonuses and you could be confused about whether there is really any difference between the commissions they claim they never pay and bonuses they actually do pay (see Figure 2)

Figure 2 – Almost all chugger recruitment ads promise bonuses and some even mention 'commission'

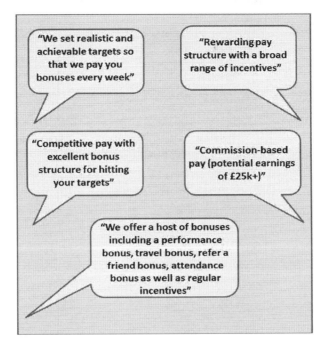

Moreover, reading the ads you might also get the impression that chuggers do have very clear daily targets and are under an awful lot of pressure to reach them. Targets for chuggers signing up direct-debit donors seem to be in the range of two to three per day.

Ad for a street F2F fundraiser - *Main Responsibilities: To raise money for the Campaign through recruitment of new donors. To consistently exceed the targets set by the Operations Manager and Campaign Lead Manager, this will normally be attaining 3 new donors per shift, per fundraiser*[19]

For chuggers trying to convince people to send small texted donations, they might be expected to recruit ten a day in their first week, rising to twenty five a day by the fourth week of their employment. In fact, chuggers' fear of missing their targets and possibly risking losing their jobs led to one case where chuggers were caught texting in small donations for each other in order to hit their texter 'sign-up' targets. Sadly for these obviously worried chuggers, software on the chugging agency's phone system recognised the chuggers' mobile phone numbers and prevented these donations from being accepted.

On the 'suckers' list'

With so many stories about identity theft and fraud appearing in the media, people have become increasingly nervous about handing over their bank details to a stranger, even to a bright, cheerful, enthusiastic, seemingly trustworthy, smiley young person wearing a suitably high-vis jacket provided by a well-known charity. However, chuggers have adapted and now often just ask potential donors to text a small donation – perhaps £2 or £3. Chuggers may even claim that this £2 or £3 will pay for food for a starving child for a week or for a sight-saving or even life-saving vaccine for a baby in Africa. This emotional pressure makes it very difficult for the person being chugged to be hard-hearted enough to refuse to give something. Many people do agree to text, either in the belief that donating this small sum really will help someone much less fortunate than themselves or else because they see it as a small price to pay to allow them to escape from the chugger. However, this £2 or £3 will seldom if ever go to the charity. In fact, were the chugger to hit their daily target of twenty to twenty five texted donations a day, these donations would hardly cover the chugger's wages for that day. Then there are still the chugging agency's fees to be paid. So, clearly there wouldn't be anything left for the charity to buy and deliver either the food for the starving child or the supposed sight-saving or life-saving vaccine.

The real aim of the £2 or £3 texted donation is not to collect the money. It's to collect the donor's phone number on the chugging agency's list of potential targets - its 'suckers list'. The chugging agency will also have, or have links with, a phone fundraising operation. Here a charity telefundraiser earning '£7.00 to £8.55 per hour plus bonuses' will call the texter and, using the fact that the texter has already apparently shown a desire to help the charity in question by texting a small amount when originally chugged in the street, try to convince them to give even more on a regular basis by setting up a direct debit for that charity.

Ad for a phone fundraiser - *The role involves calling individuals who have already expressed an interest in the campaign you are working on, and securing additional funds in a warm, friendly and persuasive manner*

And that's where the real money is made – for the fundraising agency and for the charity.

AIDA

Anyone who has ever worked in sales will immediately recognise the acronym AIDA. It stands for Attention-Interest-Decision-Action and is the basic sales process that almost all salespeople are taught to follow.[20] First you have to attract the customer's attention. Then you have to interest them in what you're trying to sell. Then comes a phase where you have to push them into making a buying decision by overcoming all their objections to buying – I don't have the money, time, need for that or whatever. And finally you want to clinch the deal – make them buy while they're still hot to trot.

Many chuggers are taught to use the AIDA sales process to get you to donate money. First they have to get your **Attention** – 'wow, nice shoes'; 'hey, want to hear my joke for today?'; 'excuse me, I think you just dropped something'; or even a straightforward 'got a couple of minutes for a chat?' are just some of the many ice-breakers a chugger might be trained to use. Apparently if you dress well, that makes you a juicy target. As an experienced chugger explained, 'people who make a lot of effort with their appearance are the easiest to pick off; they want their hair/shoes/bag noticed, so if I can deliver an ice-breaker that plays to your vanity, you'll most likely give me a few seconds'.[21]

Next is **Interest**. Now the chugger has to do a very brief but moving appeal about the charity they're collecting for that day. We also call this the 'elevator pitch' – the idea being that a chugger should be able to communicate exactly what their charity does in the time it might take them to explain this to a stranger they met while riding a few floors in an elevator. Lots of mentions of starving children, horrible diseases, sad animals, depressed donkeys, dead elephants, soon-to-be-extinct reptiles, arid deserts and so on usually do the trick. In this part of the sales process, the chugger wants to build rapport and get what they call a 'nodding donkey' – a listener who starts nodding in agreement and sympathy. As one chugging trainer emphasised, 'try to be more emotional, try not to be so factual about it'. Once a person starts to display sympathetic body language like nodding or widening their eyes or pursing their lips as they begin to consider donating, then the chugger knows they can move on to stage three – Decision.

Decision is often the trickiest bit of the sales process. It involves overcoming the target's objections to giving. There are four common objections that people tend to use with chuggers – 'I can't afford it'; 'I can't do it now'; 'I don't want to give my bank details'; and 'I already give to other charities'. This is where the salesperson, sorry I meant chugger, really displays their manipulative skill. They know in advance the main objections and they're trained how to deal with them. One explained, 'I can overcome all of these so long as I built a good rapport earlier'. One of the favourite chugger sales techniques is the 'cup of coffee a week'. If a member of the public says they can't afford to donate say £5 or £10 a month or even that they already give to other charities, the chugger might answer something like 'but it's what you'd pay for just one cup of coffee a week and for that you can feed a starving child'. The 'cup of coffee a week' trick is an excellent way of guilt-tripping a member of the public into agreeing to set up a direct debit. Or if the chugger is looking for a small £2 or £3 texted donation, they might say 'for the price of a cup of coffee you can save a child's life'.

If stages one, two and three – Attention, Interest, Decision – have been successfully completed and you've got a nodding donkey feeling guilty about their relative affluence or good health compared to the starving babies or cancer-stricken children or mistreated animals the charity is collecting for, then the final part of the sales process – **Action** (agreeing a direct debit or making a texted donation) – should be the logical next step.

Chugging rich

Chugging seems to be quite a sizeable business. About 740,000 donors signed up to direct debits in 2008-09. By 2011-12 this had risen to over 860,000 giving about £130 million a year. There are twenty to thirty fundraising companies registered with the PFRA. But there may be many others which are not registered. As for phone calls made by telefundraising agencies – just one company said it made about 1,250,000 calls a year to potential donors. That's an almost incredible 24,000 calls a week. In all, probably over ten million such calls may be made each year.

Chugging campaigns can be expensive for the charities. One campaign by Marie Curie Cancer Care cost the charity £367,000. And Shelter announced they were paying £500,000 on their drive to raise £2 million.[22] In one year, Cancer Research UK expected to pay about £3.1 million to a specialist third-party F2F fundraising agency to raise about £13.4 million from around 28,000 donors while paying the fundraising agency an average of £111 per donor.

This seems to have created a lucrative business for the chugging and telefundraising agencies. One company, set up by two former in-house charity fundraisers, made gross profits of £10.1 million on a turnover of £26.2 million and paid its two founders £2.5 million in dividends over a period of seven years, in addition to their generous salaries.

Following a spate of scandals, some charities have started to fall out of love with chugging agencies and to recruit their own in-house fundraisers. Street fundraising by charities' in-house teams shot up from 26,000 direct debits in 2009-10 to 36,000 in 2010-11 to 61,000 in 2011-12 to 73,000 in 2012-13. Moreover, some chugging agencies have closed down. One was, possibly conveniently, put into receivership just before a fundraising regulator started moves to have the company prosecuted for its dubious fundraising techniques. Then the company owning that agency packed up a few months later, but not before its two founders had become extremely wealthy thanks to the British public's generosity. However, with the exit of these two companies, one of which accounted for about a third of all street fundraising, the remaining chugging agencies seem to have full order books and potential charity clients may have to wait several months before there is an agency with capacity to handle their campaign.

Complaints, I've had a few, but then again too few to mention

There seem to be widely differing views between charity fundraisers and outsiders regarding how happy or unhappy the public are with the activities of F2F fundraisers. The charities and agencies claim they get very few complaints, 'the average complaint rate stayed very low at less than one per cent. That tells us that across the board fundraising is happening to a very high standard and proportionally generating very few complaints'.[23] However a government report found that in a survey of local authorities eighty one per cent had received complaints about the conduct of street fundraisers.[24]

When criticised about alleged harassment by its fundraisers, one tactic employed by charity industry cheerleaders has been to deflect the blame from fundraisers and instead accuse us, the public, of being tight-fisted and selfish. One charity body claimed, 'some complaints made about face to face fundraisers are not about fundraisers breaching the code of conduct but just that some people just do not like to be asked to support charity'. And a senior figure in the fundraising industry revealed his thoughts about the 'generosity' of the great British public, 'the fact that some people are offended about people asking them for money to help people who are, for the most part, in a considerably worse position just shows how messed up our society is. When you stand there as a fundraiser you get to see the bare-faced soul of the general public and I can tell you that it's not pretty. Selfishness is the epitome of evil'.[25]

Rools are for fules

Faced with a barrage of criticism about the aggressive fundraising tactics used by street chuggers, the charity industry has introduced a set of rules that chuggers should follow. These cover where chuggers should operate and who they can approach. Under the rules fundraisers must not:

- Follow a person for more than three steps
- Stand within three metres of a shop doorway, cashpoint, pedestrian crossing or station entrance
- Sign up to a Direct Debit anyone unable to give informed consent through illness, disability or drink or drugs
- Approach any members of the public who are working, such as tour guides or newspaper vendors

There are further rules governing certain information that chuggers are obliged to tell those members of the public they are targeting. Charity law makes it mandatory for chuggers to read out a 'solicitation statement' explaining how much a fundraising campaign costs and how much the charity expects to raise. This must be done before a donation is made. Reporters investigating chuggers have found that many chuggers don't make this 'solicitation statement'. With some campaigns costing hundreds of thousands of pounds, one can imagine that a chugger, desperate to reach their direct-debit sign-up or texter targets to get their bonus or even just to keep their job, might be slightly reluctant to highlight to a potential donor the vast amounts of donors' money being paid to their chugging agency.

Clampdown

Some councils seem to be getting right royally fed up with the activities of F2F fundraisers as members of the public have complained of being harassed and shopkeepers have protested that the presence of chuggers chases away their customers.

Quote: *British people gladly donate to charity in good faith, but aggressive fundraisers risk turning our high streets into an unwelcome gauntlet of bolshie bucket shakers and clip-board waving connivers.*[26]

One London councillor explained, 'businesses are extremely irritated, with potential customers crossing the road because they don't want to run the gauntlet of chuggers' and another echoed this problem, 'we are increasingly unhappy at the growing use of chuggers and the tactics they employ. They are here every day of the week and it's beginning to have a serious impact on businesses'. Over a six-week period, one survey found 543 charity fundraisers working in just the Oxford Street and Regent Street area of London's West End. But such complaints have been rejected by chugging agencies, 'fundraisers are in the streets to improve the lives of others who are considerably worse off than passers-by'. Some people may believe that they have a right to walk down their high street without being asked to donate to a charity, but the PFRA rejects this pointing out that, 'Fundraisers have rights too. They have a right to ask for a donation'.[27]

Quote: *I work in Kentish Town, and I have started to watch how many people are stopped repeatedly just walking to the Tube. Three out of ten people get stopped more than once along a 150 yard stretch. I am not uncharitable. I have a standing order to three charities. But I do object to being harassed repeatedly while going about my daily business.*

In 2012, Islington Council tried to ban chugging from six sites because 'a lot of people tell us – residents and businesses – they find this a really serious inconvenience. They feel they're harassed, a bit threatened and annoyed and we think it is something that needs to be strictly controlled'.[28] One of the council's other concerns was that only the larger charities could afford big chugging campaigns. So there was a fear that money being handed over to usually national chugging charities would lead to less money being given to local charities. But the council found that it didn't have the powers to prevent chugging.

In 2014, Birmingham City Council tried to pass a bye-law banning chuggers from the city centre. But this was blocked by the Government because, as the Local Government Minister explained, 'councils should be tough and rigid where this has got out of hand, but creating laws so that nobody can fundraise ever isn't the way to do it'.[29]

Around 250 councils have signed agreements with the PFRA giving the councils some control over the amount of and nature of the chugging in their areas and this appears to have led to a fall in complaints. But street chugging may have annoyed so many people that it's becoming increasingly unproductive and may already have passed its peak. So charities are moving on to something that appears to be much more effective – door-stepping us.

From high street to your street

Although chugging is possibly the fundraising method that has received the most negative publicity, it actually accounts for quite a small proportion - 125,827 of the 726,494 F2F direct debits recruited in 2012-13. That's just seventeen percent. The other eighty three per cent of direct debits (600,667) were recruited by door-to-door (D2D) fundraisers. In fact, street chugging is declining, dropping by forty seven per cent between 2011-12 and 2012-13 from 238,273 direct debits to 125,827. Moreover, the number of 'prospecting sites' used by street fundraisers also fell from 5,423 to just 3,516. Over the same period, D2D direct debits only went down four per cent from 625,134 to 600,667. So it would seem that attempts by councils to control chugging are forcing chuggers off our high streets and on to the streets where we live.

The scale of door-stepping might seem surprising. There were a fairly impressive thirty one million solicitations in 2010 rising 72 per cent to forty three million in 2012. With just over 600,000 direct debits being recruited in 2012, that meant around seventy households have to be disturbed for every one direct debit recruited.

Critics of D2D fundraising have suggested that it is much easier for fundraisers to pressure, harass and bully people at their homes as the targets cannot just walk away as they could if stopped by a chugger in the street.

Some people may even end up agreeing a direct debit just to get rid of the door-stepper. But several charities have rejected these criticisms. Scope, a disability charity helping people with cerebral palsy explained, 'Door-to-door fundraising is a very effective method of raising money and attracts long-term support particularly from younger donors'. Scope also reassured us that all its door-to-door representatives are 'subjected to a rigorous selection process and undergo intensive training'. But it's possible that not all door-steppers, and particularly commission- or bonus-based fundraisers from agencies, are quite as rigorously selected and intensively trained as those from Scope as the number of complaints about harassment from door-steppers rose by 93 per cent from 2,877 in 2011 to 5,555 in 2012.

Quote: *He told me he had just lost his wife and could not afford to sign up. But the team leader who was listening said I should have pushed him further after he said no. They said 'look at his house. He can afford it'. I was just shocked. I did not expect this from a charity.*

Chapter 5

Playing Politics

It's war!

In the middle of June 2014 there was a major outbreak of hostilities. This was not in the Ukraine, nor in Iraq. This was in Britain and it was between the charity sector and its supporters on one side and the Conservative Party on the other. The flashpoint seems to have been the publication by Oxfam of a report titled *'The Perfect Storm: Economic stagnation, the rising cost of living, public spending cuts, and the impact on UK poverty'*. In its report, Oxfam made a number of claims which understandably somewhat upset the Tories. For example Oxfam wrote, 'the economy is stagnating, unemployment is increasing, prices are rising, incomes are falling, and spending on public services is being cut back rapidly'. In addition, the Oxfam report threw out some fairly spine-chilling statistics - 13.5 million people live in poverty in Britain; the 'UK is one of the most unequal rich countries in the world'; 5.5 million UK households are affected by fuel poverty; the 'UK has weaker protection for those in work than Mexico' and so on. Oxfam accompanied its report with a tweeted mocked-up film poster. Several times I've asked Oxfam for permission to include a copy of its poster and tweet in my book and each time Oxfam has refused. So, I'll have to describe the mocked-up film poster as I'm not allowed to show it. The poster depicted a rough, foaming, tempestuous sea under a dark, gloomy, threatening sky and the 'film' title – THE PERFECT STORM. Underneath the title was the text:

Starring:

ZERO HOUR CONTRACTS

HIGH PRICES

BENEFIT CUTS

UNEMPLOYMENT

CHILDCARE COSTS

Some people might wonder why Oxfam seems to have adopted a fairly low profile when unemployment shot up by a shocking 55 per cent from 1.62 million to 2.51 million from 2007 to 2010 under New Labour, while energy and food prices also rocketed. Yet Oxfam launched its campaign against poverty in the UK while unemployment was falling by 17 per cent from 2.51 million to 2.08 million under the Coalition and while, in spite of Oxfam's and the Government's claims of public-spending cuts, public spending was still rising seemingly inexorably. Though Oxfam's claims that many of the supposedly newly created jobs were part-time, people on zero-hours contracts and people working for themselves as they couldn't get a proper job may have some justification.

Whatever the truth behind the unemployment statistics, the extent of poverty and the trajectory of public spending, Oxfam's rather negative message seemed to directly contradict the Conservatives' upbeat message at the time that they had successfully turned the economy around, created record numbers of new jobs and 'helped unleash Britain's entrepreneurial spirit'.[30] A government spokesperson cast doubt on Oxfam's claims, 'I think they'll find unemployment is falling, that we've just taken action over zero-hour contracts, and that there was a Childcare Bill in the Queen's Speech which will offer tax-free childcare to all parents with kids under 12 by autumn 2015 and cover 85 per cent of childcare costs of those families receiving universal credit'.[31]

Faced with criticism, Oxfam of course defended itself and stressed its impartiality, 'Oxfam is a resolutely non-party political organisation - we have a duty to draw attention to the hardship suffered by poor people we work with in the UK. Fighting poverty should not be a party political issue - successive governments have presided over a tide of rising inequality and created a situation where food banks and other providers provided 20 million meals last year to people who could not afford to feed themselves'.[32]

But the Conservatives seemed unconvinced. One senior Tory wrote, 'Oxfam has stated that its campaign is not politically motivated, but the fact that it is so willing to ignore the positive news in the economy and refuse to take a balanced position shows that it has allowed itself to become a mouthpiece for the political left'. She went on to question Oxfam's silence when new Labour crashed the economy in the magnificent Brown and Balls Bust, 'because it was so silent under Labour when the economy was worsening, its claims of political impartiality now have little or no credibility'. Another stated, 'many people who support Oxfam will be shocked and saddened by this highly political campaigning in domestic British politics. I cannot see how using funds donated to charity to campaign politically can be in accord with Oxfam's charitable status'.[33]

The row soon died down. But a couple of months later, the whole issue blew up again when the new Tory Minister for Civil Society, who grew up in both the US and the UK, suggested 'what charities should be doing is sticking to their knitting' and charities should be 'doing the best they can to promote their agenda which should be about helping others'.[34] The phrase 'sticking to their knitting' probably wasn't intended to refer to little old ladies busily knitting things to be sold at charity fundraising events. In fact, it was most likely a reference to an idea made popular by American management gurus Tom Peters and Robert H. Waterman, Jr. in their 1982 multi-million copy bestseller *In Search Of Excellence*. In the book, the authors identified the main characteristics of successful companies. One was that they did what the authors called 'stick to the knitting' – they stay with businesses they understand, rather than being tempted by empire-building to create large conglomerates spanning many industries by buying up businesses in other sectors as many large companies had done in the 1960s and 1970s. But perhaps not understanding the allusion to management theory rather than frantically knitting grannies, charity standard-bearers quickly and furiously described the minister's comments as 'incredibly insulting', 'sexist' and 'dismissive'.

Government to burn witches?

Also in 2014, we had the great badger bust-up. This time it was between the RSPCA and the Conservatives. When the Secretary of State for the Environment announced restarting a badger cull as part of the Government's effort to save cattle from tuberculosis that led to over 37,000 cattle being slaughtered in 2012 and a further 32,620 killed in 2013, the RSPCA swung into action. The farmers involved should be 'named and shamed' the chief executive of the RSPCA demanded as 'those who care will not want to visit areas or buy milk from farms soaked in badgers' blood'.[35] Moreover a year earlier at the start of the first badger cull, a former rock guitarist, who was against the badger cull, opined that killing badgers 'under the dishonest pretext of "vermin control"' would set 'the value of every wild mammal at zero'.[36] He was also quoted as saying, 'there is no reason to suppose that it would stop there. We may see a return to legalised badger-baiting, bear-baiting and even the burning of supposed witches at the stake'.[37] And he warned us, 'Britain at this point either allows Cameron's government to propel us back into the Dark Ages of barbarism, or we all stand up and cry "No!"'.

The badger bust-up was not the first run-in the RSPCA had with the political elites. In 2012 the charity hit the headlines when it spent around £326,000 of supporters' donations prosecuting David Cameron's local hunt, the Heythrop Hunt in Oxfordshire, for allegedly breaking anti-hunting laws. In spite of having its own in-house legal department, the RSPCA engaged three barristers and a solicitors' firm and managed to rack up more than seven times as much in legal fees than was spent by the defendants. In this case, a cross-party group of MPs and Lords reported the RSPCA to the Charity Commission for breaching a 'duty of prudence by the trustees of the RSPCA in that it cannot possibly be argued that charitable funds and assets have been used reasonably'.[38] The RSPCA's critics also complained that had the RSPCA handed over its evidence to the Crown Prosecution Service (CPS), the CPS could have chosen to prosecute the hunt had the public interest requirement been met, thus saving RSPCA supporters £326,000.

Over the following twelve months, the RSPCA continued its assault on hunters bringing (unsuccessful) prosecutions against the Cheshire Hunt, the Cheshire Forest Hunt and the Ledbury Hunt. Though two of nine summonses brought by the RSPCA against the Avon Vale Hunt in Wiltshire did result in convictions and a member of the Seavington Hunt in Somerset was convicted and fined £500. A member of the Countryside Alliance accused the RSPCA of issuing the summonses as part of a political campaign against hunting that was an 'abuse of the courts'. And in a leaked internal document, the RSPCA's deputy chairman warned, 'there is a potential risk, which does not seem to have been identified or addressed, that if the society is seen to become too "political", that ....new and existing partners may become concerned that their own brand could be affected negatively by being associated with us'.[39]

Politics R Us

Many other charities have also been tempted away from their main focus on relieving suffering into campaigning to change attitudes and the law. Christian Aid has been criticised for bias in favour of the Palestinians and against the Israelis. Moreover, in 2013 Christian Aid staff joined with ACT Alliance and other global partners at the United Nations Rio+20 summit in Brazil to lobby the UK government on sustainable energy, clamping down on tax avoidance and the concept of a green economy. Also in 2013, Christian Aid sent its Tax Justice Bus round the country. By the end of its 53-day tour of Britain and Ireland, more than 5,000 people – including 56 MPs – had climbed aboard to hear how tax dodging hurts people both here at home and in the world's poorest countries. During the tour, 10,000 people signed the Tick for Tax Justice action cards, which called on Prime Minister David Cameron to use his global leadership to tackle tax dodging. Many donors to Christian Aid might be surprised to learn that their money was being used to campaign against supposed Anthropogenic Global Warming or Climate Change or whatever it's called by the time this book is published, to campaign for higher planet-saving green taxes on our energy bills and to pay for a touring bus demanding a clampdown on tax avoidance. However much ordinary citizens may want to pay a lot more for their energy and however laudable a crackdown on tax cheats may be, it's possible that this is not what Christian Aid's supporters believe the charity should be using their money for.

The much loved Save the Children also got slightly burnt when it tried its hand at politics. Save the Children is generally associated with its work helping starving children in Africa and other Third World regions. But in 2012 it launched a TV campaign in Britain to raise £500,000 to help children in poverty in Britain. The ad featured a boy called Alex whose parents didn't eat proper meals in order to save money. In the ad Alex also wasn't getting much food as he only has toast for breakfast and a sandwich for dinner. While most charity appeals showing children in poverty abroad feature real scenes from famine-hit or war-blighted areas of the world, this Save the Children ad used extremely photogenic actors. At the same time, Save the Children published a report full of shocking statistics about the supposed level of child poverty in Britain. One of Save the Children's claims that 1.6 million British children were living in poverty was widely reported by the BBC. But a subsequent BBC investigation concluded the figures used by Save the Children were 'utter rubbish'.[40] Critics attacked Save the Children's apparent political bias. One Conservative MP perhaps predictably said, 'I'm a supporter of Save the Children and I am becoming increasingly concerned about their political involvement and about the people who are getting involved in them, seemingly with a political agenda'.[41] Though the charity issued the usual rebuttal, 'it is a shame that some critics want to divert attention from the powerful insight our campaign has given into the lives of the very poorest children in Britain today'.[42]

Fake charities

In 2012 a couple of bloggers had a look at Britain's massive charity industry. The bloggers noticed that 'more and more charities were being cited by the news media – and, most especially, the BBC' as part of news stories. The media likes to interview people from charities as they are generally much more trusted by the public than business leaders, trade unionists, journalists or politicians (see Figure 1)

Figure 1 - Charities are reasonably trusted by the public

How much do you trust to tell the truth?*	
Doctors	89%
Teachers	86%
Armed forces	70%
Clergy & priests	66%
Police	65%
Charities	56% ⬅
Trade unions	41%
Business leaders	34%
Estate agents	24%
Bankers	21%
Journalists	21%
Politicians	18%

* Source Ipsos Mori and nfpSynergy

Being presented in the media as coming from a charity creates a kind of halo effect as most people believe charities work for 'good causes'. Although, while trust in charities was at 56 per cent in 2014, surveys suggest that trust was at 66 per cent a year earlier. It seems to have fallen quite dramatically over just one year following several newspaper articles about the allegedly over-generous salaries paid to some charity bosses.

The problem the bloggers identified was that many of the charities most often interviewed and quoted by the media were actually campaigning organisations which frequently called for policies 'that aimed to reduce freedom and liberty in this country'. So the bloggers decided to investigate where some of these charities got their money and how they spent it. They then came up with the idea of 'fake charities'. They defined fake charities as 'any organisation registered as a UK charity that derives more than ten per cent of its income – and/or more than £1 million – from the Government, while also lobbying the Government. That lobbying can take the form of calling for new policies, changes to the law or increases in (their own) funding'.

Many members of the public probably imagine that most charities are organisations funded largely by private donations – a bit like the RNLI. But the Fake Charity bloggers estimated that around 27,000 British charities were dependent on the Government for three quarters or more of their funding. Without our Government handing over mountains of taxpayers' cash, a large number of these charities would probably collapse.

Quote: *Among members of the public who give generously to charity, it's perhaps not widely understood how many charities have become, probably without any alternative, more dependent on government, and this should be aired and discussed*[43]

Moreover, the bloggers found that many of these charities spent much of their time and money lobbying politicians and the Government to change the law to support their particular cause rather than doing what most people would consider 'charitable work' – helping the poor or the sick, saving people from starvation, educating disadvantaged or Third World children, looking after animals and so on.

There seem to be two parts to the fake charity description – firstly taking an awful lot of taxpayers' money and secondly using this money for political campaigning rather than genuine charitable work.

The double-dippers

There are many charities that do a great deal of real charitable work, but also receive a perhaps surprising amount of our money directly from the Government while in addition asking us for many millions or even tens of millions more in private donations. We could call these charities the 'double-dippers', because they get two chances to extract money from us – firstly straight from our taxes in the form of government grants and then again through usually heart-rending fundraising campaigns to get us to donate. Some of the anti-poverty charities are particularly successful at this double-dipping. Oxfam, for example picked up almost £137 million from taxpayers in Britain and abroad during the last year. That's around 37 per cent of its total revenue of £368 million. Save the Children also got close to £137 million from taxpayers – 48 per cent of its income of £284 million. And Christian Aid was given about £39 million – 41 per cent of its funds – from governments being admirably generous with taxpayers' cash (see Figure 2)

Figure 2 – Some anti-poverty charities are given tens of millions of pounds from the taxes we pay

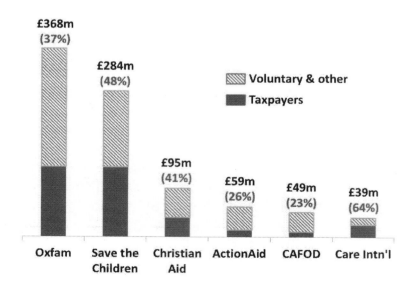

In their annual reports, our charities have different ways of classifying the receipt of millions or even tens of millions of pounds of taxpayers' money. Some charities openly call this money 'government grants'. But others refer to this money as 'voluntary income' – although it's not clear that all taxpayers were aware of their own magnanimity when their governments made these 'voluntary' donations on their behalf. Moreover, one could suspect that ordinary members of the public believe that the taxes they pay are mostly used to fund public services like schools, roads, hospitals, the military and the police and don't actually realise that their favourite charity may already be getting tens of millions of pounds from them via the Government. In fact, one could imagine that if they knew how much taxpayers' money some charities were already receiving, many people might feel rather less inclined to hand over another £5 or £10 a month directly from their own already heavily-taxed wages or pensions. For example, an Oxfam collector who said something like, 'Oxfam already gets almost £137 million of the money you pay in tax, but we would really like you to set up a direct debit for another £10 a month to help starving African children' probably wouldn't end up with too many willing donors.

The freedom-fighters

There is another group of possibly 'fake charities' which not only take sizeable amounts of our tax money, but also seem to do very little in the way of what most of us would consider as 'charitable activities'. In fact, many of them spend almost all their time and money doing things like 'raising awareness' and 'influencing opinion-leaders' and lobbying either for changes in the law, usually to restrict our freedoms, and/or for extra taxes on activities that these fake charities consider to be harmful to ourselves or the environment. There's nothing wrong with campaigning and influencing and lobbying for new laws and taxes. Any group should be allowed to campaign for any cause in which it believes. But the issue is whether an organisation that is mainly focused on these campaigning activities deserves to promulgate its opinions under the banner or even halo of being a 'charity' while at the same time using its charitable status to avoid paying any tax on its income.

With many people the word 'charity' conjures up images of independence and voluntary donations to selfless grass-roots organisations working for the common good. But most of these fake charities are far from independent; are not supported by much of society, otherwise they could survive without government hand-outs; and are engaged in imposing their views on the rest of us whether we agree with them or not. Many are wedded to one ideological viewpoint – banning smoking, minimum pricing on alcohol, increasing energy taxes, reducing speed limits and so on – and tend to push their viewpoint as if they were genuinely reflecting public opinion. In a way, most of these fake charities, while claiming to be mouthpieces of grass-roots democracy, are subverting the democratic process and are engaged in social engineering by masquerading either as public opinion or else as being experts who know what is best for us, usually without ever actually consulting us. Some of their causes such as higher taxes, greater regulation, increasing foreign aid, abstinence from alcohol, identity politics and the creation of costly new quangos to enforce their new laws may even be unpopular with wide sections of the public. This may be why, in spite of calling themselves 'charities', most are able to raise little to nothing in the way of money donated by any members of the public. So they have to rely on government giving them our money to pay for them to lobby government to change the law to suit their own political or social agendas.

Some of the areas where these fake charities are most active are in fighting against smoking, alcohol, junk food, motorists and what they perceive as inequality.

In the anti-smoking lobby, probably the most vociferous and effective organisation is ASH (Action on Smoking and Health). ASH is very clear that it is a campaigning group. In its 2013 report it states: 'ASH is an organisation which provides information on all aspects of tobacco and works to advance policies and measures that will help to prevent the addiction, disease and unnecessary premature death caused by smoking'. And in listing its successes for 2013, ASH wrote, 'this was another important year for ASH. Once again ASH has provided excellent leadership in building support for implementation of the Government's Tobacco Control Plan and the campaign for plain, standardised tobacco packaging'. In 2013, of its £752,746 income ASH was given £150,000 from the Department of Health, £447,074 from other charities, £125,000 from one legacy and possibly only around £6,000 from voluntary donations. So, however worthy ASH's intentions, it's not obvious that it is a charity whose purposes are widely supported by an enthusiastic public desperately eager to donate their own money to ASH's noble cause.

Helping improve the food we eat, we have quite a few charities including the Children's Food Trust, SUSTAIN, the Obesity Forum, Weight Concern and CASH (Consensus Action on Salt and Health).

The Children's Food Trust 'exists to help protect every child's right to eat better – and so, to do better'. It seems that all of the Children's Food Trust's £4,239,000 came from the Government or from other charities.

SUSTAIN is active in many areas of improving the quality of our food, especially food in hospitals and for children. Just £33,173 of SUSTAIN's £2,094,720 revenue appears to be from voluntary income. Amongst many other presumably worthy activities, SUSTAIN used some of its (mostly taxpayers') money to launch a number of mostly unsuccessful complaints to the Advertising Standards Authority (ASA) complaining about the promotion of Swizzels and about the way games featuring the Haribo Super Mix Challenge, Chewie the Chewits dinosaur and the Sugar Puffs Honey Monster allegedly encouraged children to eat excessive amounts of products that were bad for their health.

Weight Concern's goal is to 'address the physical and psychological needs of overweight people' and it aims to 'provide a voice for those who have first-hand experience of being overweight in the UK'. It seems to get about £5,154 of its £59,822 income from donations.

CASH tries 'to persuade the food processors and suppliers to universally and gradually reduce the salt content of processed foods'. CASH has been very successful in campaigning to reduce the salt content in food. In just one year, the Food Standards Agency spent £3.47 million of our taxes on a 'salt awareness campaign'. Perhaps sadly for CASH and the Food Standards Agency, a series of studies completed in 2014 concluded that the 'focus on salt had been misguided' and that 'researchers had overplayed the extent to which reduced salt intake could account for the reduction in fatalities from heart disease and strokes'.[44] In 2013 CASH generated around £4,563 – about three per cent - of its £141,335 income from voluntary donations.

With the fight against alcohol, we have Alcohol Concern 'leading the campaign against cheap alcohol and pressing the Government to take action through different policies such as a minimum price for alcohol and tougher licensing laws'.[45] In 2013, of its £1,026,828 income, Alcohol Concern received £222,298 as a grant from the Department from Education and another £225,626 from the Welsh Assembly Government. Most of the charity's other income came from consultancy and training. From the annual report, it's difficult to find any voluntary donations at all from ordinary members of the public to this campaigning charity where the average employee cost for its twelve staff was a quite generous £37,368 in 2013.

The Institute of Alcohol Studies' aim is 'to educate and to preserve and protect the good health of the public by promoting the scientific understanding of beverage alcohol and the individual, social and health consequences of its consumption'. In 2013, £309,208 (98.7 per cent) of the charity's £313,252 income came from just one grant from one organisation – the Alliance House Foundation. The objectives of the Alliance House Foundation are 'to spread the principles of total abstinence from alcoholic drinks and to promote the moral and physical welfare of the community'. Also helping fund research into the destructive effects of alcohol is Alcohol Research UK. Around £545,000 of its £703,000 income appears to come from investments with most of the rest coming from other charities such as the Drinkaware Trust and Alcohol Health Network. It's not obvious that there are any voluntary donations from any members of the public to this charity.

The great green cash grab

Perhaps the area affecting us all where there are more charities than you can shake a stick at is protecting the environment and in particular saving us all from the catastrophe/bogeyman/fraud (delete as appropriate) of Anthropogenic Global Warming. Here we British taxpayers willingly pour our money into the bank accounts of organisations like Forum for the Future, Friends of the Earth, Global Action Plan, Green Alliance, Low Carbon Communities Network, New Economics Foundation and the Women's Environmental Network to name just a few.

Most of these green charities support policies like increased taxes on our energy bills, decarbonising our energy supply, building more wind farms and solar farms, restricting motoring and so on. Moreover, these charities have been very successful in influencing government policy. Their greatest success was probably in 2008 when the then Environment Secretary Ed Miliband's Climate Change Act was passed into law by 463 votes to three, at the same time as the snow was falling outside the Houses of Parliament during what even the *Guardian* later admitted was the coldest year since 2000.[46] By the Government's own estimate, it would cost £404 billion to implement the Climate Change Act – £760 per household every year for four decades. Moreover, the Act would lead to the destruction of tens of thousands of jobs as energy-intensive industries like steelworks, oil refineries, aluminium smelting and many chemical plants would no longer be able to operate profitably in Britain due to the Act's imposition of higher energy taxes than in many other countries. The Act, probably misguidedly, included a voluntary commitment to reduce Britain's carbon dioxide emissions by 80 per cent of their 1990 level by 2050 – a target generally acknowledged to be achievable only by shutting down most of the economy – in an effort to demonstrate Britain's 'global leadership'. In spite of the claims of our green charities to represent public opinion, it's far from obvious that the majority of British citizens support the charities' plans to push up energy prices and possibly cripple our economy in order to save the planet, especially when the UK is only responsible for about 1.47 per cent of man-made CO2 emissions.

Blame Blair?

Britain's charities haven't always been so politically active. Prior to the arrival of New Labour, any form of political lobbying by a charity or campaigning to have laws changed could only be 'incidental or ancillary to its charitable purpose' and could not be a charity's 'dominant' activity. But in 2002, the Prime Minister's Strategy Unit advocated a loosening of the rules because 'charities perform a valuable role in campaigning for social change'. The Strategy Unit proposed 'the guidelines on campaigning should be revised to encourage charities to play this role to the fullest extent'.[47] Sure enough in 2004 an obedient Charity Commission changed its rules to allow charities to engage in non-party political campaigning provided this activity was not 'the dominant method by which the organisation will pursue its apparently charitable objects'.[48]

In 2007, there was another government request for further relaxation of restrictions on charities' political campaigning. A Cabinet Office study recommended that charities should have the right to conduct political campaigns and went so far as to propose that even organisations whose whole purpose was political should be allowed to be accorded charitable status. The Charity Commission wouldn't go quite as far as New Labour wished by allowing purely political organisations to be classed as charities. But in 2008 it did further loosen its rules allowing charitable status for organisations for whom political campaigning was the 'dominant' activity but not including those for whom political campaigning was 'the continuing and sole activity' or those that were too openly party political. But then the Commission provided a get-out-of-jail-free card to political charities by agreeing that a charity could 'direct all of its resources towards legislative targets', though only 'for a period'. However, the Commission didn't define how long this 'period' should be. This pretty much created an 'anything goes' for our charities. Britain's new laissez faire approach encouraged by New Labour contrasted very strongly with the policy of regulatory authorities in the US. In the US, by law political campaigning could be no more than an 'insubstantial' part of a charity's activities. In the UK, on the other hand, even an insubstantial amount of charitable activity was enough for a campaigning group to qualify for registration as a charity.[49]

Possibly concerned by the growing extent of political campaigning by charities and other bodies, in January 2014 the Coalition introduced the Transparency of Lobbying, Non-party Campaigning and Trade Union Administration Bill. The aims of the Bill were quite modest. It only required that in the short period from the dissolution of Parliament up to a general election, campaigning groups should register their spending with the Electoral Commission if it exceeded more than £450,000 across the whole of the UK or more than £9,750 in any single constituency. This £450,000 was a reduction from the previous level of £988,000.

These proposals were met with howls of anguished fury by many charities and their apologists. One called the Bill the 'charity gagging bill'. The Bill would have 'a chilling effect on democracy' the leader of a major charity ominously warned. 'This is a bad day for anyone wanting to protect the environment, save a hospital or oppose tuition fees' claimed a Friends of the Earth spokeswoman. Oxfam complained that the new rules would 'unduly restrict the ability of charities and others to speak out on issues of legitimate concern'. While another major campaigning charity warned 'these tight new spending caps, and the much broader range of activities caught by those caps, will make it all but impossible for charities to work collaboratively on many issues that are important to the public and the planet'. And a charity insider accused the Government of 'running a campaign seeking to intimidate social welfare charities'.

But the Charity Commission seemed to suggest that some charities were possibly over-reacting and that there really was no need for their furious explosions of rage, 'charity law makes it quite clear that political activity and campaigning can be legitimate and valuable activities for charities to undertake as a way of furthering their charitable purposes. The legislation changes the rules that apply in the run-up to general elections, but does not challenge the important principle that charities are free to campaign, so long as they do so to further their mission'.[50] Moreover, an MP supporting the bill rejected the charities' outrage, 'if a member of the public puts a pound in a rattling tin, and that money is spent on press officers and Bell Pottinger to lobby a bunch of politicians, wouldn't that person feel a bit disgusted and a bit cheated?' And another wondered what all the fuss was about, 'as most donors to charities would expect their money to be spent on good works rather than party politics this (the Bill) is both reasonable and hardly changed from the current situation'.

Quote: *Think charity and you think of the volunteer rattling a tin, front-line work relieving poverty and vocation lined with compassion. You don't think of political campaigning. Yet in too many cases this has become the culture of the charitable sector. And it needs to change*[51]

Chapter 6

The foreign aid farrago

Send more money!

The figures for worldwide poverty are shocking. About three billion people – just under half of the World's population - live on less than $2.50 a day; 22,000 children a day – over eight million a year – die due to the effects poverty (malnutrition and disease); one in three children (640 million) live without adequate shelter; one in five children (400 million) don't have access to safe water; one in seven children (270 million) don't have access to healthcare.

Given these ghastly statistics you'd think that nobody with any humanity could oppose increasing the amount of foreign aid we should give to those so much less fortunate than ourselves. In 1970, a group of developed countries agreed at the UN to increase their foreign aid contributions to 0.7 per cent of their Gross National Income (GNI) and then all but three rich Scandinavian countries conveniently forgot about this commitment.

Figure 1 – Global foreign aid almost doubled between 2003 and 2011, but has fallen slightly since then

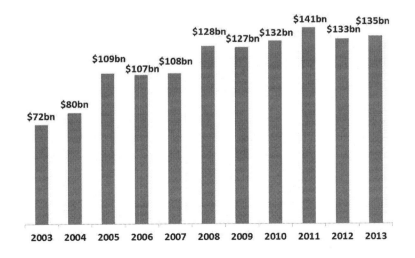

Nevertheless, the amount the world's richest countries give in aid has been going up significantly – from around $72 billion in 2003 to $135 billion in 2013 – an 87 per cent increase in only a decade (see Figure 1)

Britain has long been more generous than most other First World countries with our foreign aid running at around 0.56 per cent of GNI. However for Britain, things changed with the arrival of the Conservative/LibDem Coalition. The Coalition proudly announced that, in spite of cuts being made to public spending at home, UK foreign aid would shoot up from 0.56 per cent of GNI to the agreed UN target of 0.7 per cent. This made increasingly heavily-indebted Britain the fourth most generous provider of foreign aid in terms of aid as a percentage of GNI (see Figure 2)

Figure 2 – Only three small, rich Scandinavian countries give more foreign aid as a percentage of GNI than the UK

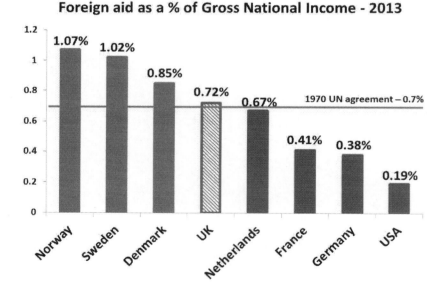

Just between 2010 when the Coalition came to power and 2013, Britain's foreign aid rocketed by around 45 per cent from about £7.8 billion a year to £11.3 billion by 2013. Foreign aid now costs each household in the UK £428 a year. This enabled Britain to achieve the Coalition's bold ambition of becoming a 'global aid superpower'. Sadly for those of us living in Britain, at the same time that Britain was becoming ever more of a 'global aid superpower' it was becoming ever less of a global economic superpower due to the Coalition increasing the country's national debt from around £700 billion in 2010 to about £1.3 trillion by 2013 and to over £1.4 trillion by the 2015 general election. It may be interesting to note that just the £3.5 billion increase in Britain's foreign aid spending under the Coalition would have been more than sufficient to pay for the 39,500 military and 32,400 police plus support staff who were losing their jobs in Britain as part of the Coalition's public-spending cuts in its totally futile attempts to 'balance the country's books'.

So, in spite of having almost the fastest increasing level of national debt in the world, in terms of total dollars in foreign aid, little Britain suddenly shot up to become the second most generous country in the world, with the massive USA taking the number one spot. Perhaps surprisingly, Britain now gives much more in aid each year than considerably wealthier Germany (see Figure 3)

Figure 3 – Britain has the second highest foreign aid budget in the world

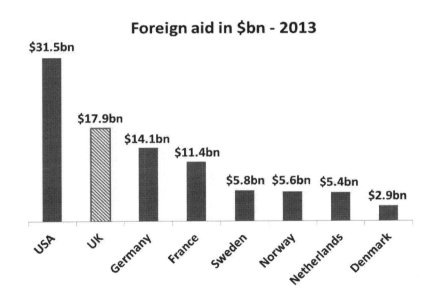

The poverty problem

When most people think of foreign aid, they tend to imagine brave aid workers rescuing people from earthquakes, tsunamis, floods, famines and other such natural disasters. But this emergency aid accounts for an extremely small part of the foreign aid money we give either directly to charities or through our taxes to charities and various relief agencies. Perhaps just $5 billion to $6 billion of the $135 billion a year foreign aid is emergency aid. The other ninety five or so per cent of charity and aid money goes to what's called 'development aid' – helping countries escape from poverty and putting them on the path to development.

In the last sixty years around $3 trillion has been donated by developed countries to help poorer countries. There have been some major successes – extreme poverty has been more than halved, diseases like river blindness and smallpox have been all but eradicated and millions of lives have been saved from famine and conflict. Moreover, many aid recipients have managed to break free from poverty and achieve rising levels of prosperity for their people. In the 1960s countries like Malaysia, Indonesia, China, Thailand, South Korea and Taiwan had lower income per capita than some African countries. Now, thanks in part to aid, they have shot ahead of their African counterparts. South Korea for example, used to have a lower income per capita than Ghana. By 2013 South Korea's income per capita at $33,189 was close to ten times that of Ghana at just $3,461. Though the country which has achieved most in improving the lot of its population is probably China where, with very little foreign aid at all, close to seven hundred million people have been taken out of poverty in just thirty years.

But while most formerly poor Asian and some South American countries have made significant progress on the road to development and modernisation, too many countries, particularly in Africa, have stagnated or even become more impoverished over the last few decades in spite of being given more in aid than any other part of the world. In Europe, after the Second World War the US-sponsored Marshall Plan is generally credited for helping war-ravaged European countries to rebuild and become prosperous. So some people have demanded a 'Marshall Plan for Africa'. There's only one problem with this demand. Africa has already had its Marshall Plan – several times over. In the last fifty years Africa has been given the equivalent of around ten Marshall Plans. In today's money, the five-year European Marshall Plan saw about $100 billion - $20 billion a year - being used to rebuild Europe after WWII. In the last fifty years, Africa has received over $1 trillion in aid. So, Africa received about the same every year - $20 billion a year - for fifty years that Europe received each year for just five years. Yet there's little evidence that those countries getting the most aid have benefited from this aid and a quarter of Sub-Saharan countries, including some of the world's recipients of the most foreign aid, are now poorer than they were in 1960.

Quote: *The notion that aid can eliminate systemic poverty, and has done so, is a myth. Millions in Africa are poorer today because of aid; misery and poverty have not ended but have increased.*[52]

Similarly in the last ten years just one country, Afghanistan with a population of only thirty million, has had around $100 billion in foreign aid – a full Marshall Plan. Yet it's far from obvious that much, if anything has been achieved. And there's certainly been nothing like the progress seen in Europe after the devastation of WWII.

The failure of too many countries to benefit from the vast amounts of aid they have received has led to some people beginning to question the last sixty years' dogma that by giving ever more money we can make poverty history. While sometimes tax-dodging multi-millionaire rock-stars and film celebrities have hung out with presidents and prime ministers enthusiastically lecturing us about the need to give ever more of our money to help the poor in the Third World, there have been several influential books such as *The Trouble with Africa: Why foreign aid isn't working, It's Our Turn to Eat,* and *Dead Aid: Why aid is not working and there is another way for Africa* which have suggested that pouring ever larger amounts of money into foreign aid budgets may not be the right way to help the impoverished and the destitute. These books have been written, not by rabid, Ayn-Randish, right-wing, free-market extremists, but by people who care deeply about how our aid money is spent, or too often mis-spent, and who possibly have more experience and more knowledge of the foreign aid industry than extremely wealthy, media-attention-grabbing rock idols and multi-millionaire Hollywood superstars.

The development aid industry is huge. It employs at least 500,000 people worldwide and spends close to $130 billion of developed countries' taxpayers' money. It has been extremely successful at not only fighting off any attempts to control its spending, but also at cloaking itself in moral righteousness as it demands ever more of our money to help the ever fewer countries that are still trapped in poverty.

Quote: *From my time in Africa, it was the international tax-free charity workers that drove the new Land Cruisers, Land Rovers and shiny Mercedes and who worked in the smartest buildings. It was also these workers who lived in the very smart areas with government ministers as neighbours*[53]

Given the failure of many African and a few South American countries to benefit from eye-wateringly large amounts of foreign aid, there have been furious disputes about the effectiveness of foreign aid between those riding the often lucrative foreign aid gravy train - the 'lords of poverty' - and critics of the way aid money is used. The lords of poverty tend to claim that even if some aid is wasted, the more we give, the more lives we will save and the more people will be taken out of poverty. But critics have argued that there is no proven correlation between the amount of aid given and recipient countries' growth. However this is probably a futile debate. The truth may be that some countries – European countries after WWII, many Asian countries and some South American countries – have had a history, culture and forms of government which have enabled them to take advantage of the aid they have received. But there are also too many other countries which have turned out to be foreign aid bottomless pits, have not moved forward in spite of massive aid spending and may now require a completely different approach if they are to ever escape from the poverty trap.

This new approach means understanding the mechanics of how countries develop. Although China has grown largely without foreign aid, it perhaps gives a good insight into at least three conditions which must be in place for a country to improve the lives of its citizens:

1. Population growth must be lower than economic growth if people are to become wealthier
2. Corruption must be contained and money extracted by corruption reinvested in the country rather than being siphoned off to international tax havens
3. The 'resource curse' or 'aid curse' must be carefully managed so that a country's economy doesn't become unbalanced enriching the few connected with the resource while impoverishing the rest.

1. The population explosion

It is surely common sense that if a country's population grows at a faster rate than the economy, then on average people will become poorer. And no country can possibly become richer while its people are gradually impoverished. Obvious as this is, it seems that this truism is repeatedly ignored by most of the lords of poverty. The problem is probably that political correctness and the fear of being seen as neo-colonialists have prevented most aid organisations from appearing to dictate the kinds of policies aid recipients should implement. The result has been disastrous.

In 1984, the song *'Do They Know It's Christmas?'* was released by Band Aid to raise money to help the starving victims of the 1983-85 Ethiopian famine. The record plus the following year's Live Aid concert raised around £150 million and made those behind the venture into national heroes. In 1965, eighteen years before the start of the famine, the population of Ethiopia was about twenty five million. In 1984, in the midst of the famine, the country's population had passed thirty nine million.

Figure 4 – The populations of famine-hit Ethiopia and Sudan have increased rapidly

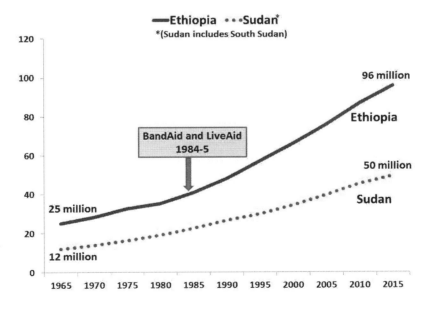

Today, Ethiopia's population is around ninety six million – well over twice the level during the 1983-85 famine and almost four times the population in 1965. There have been similar situations in two other neighbouring African countries where there are regular famines – Somalia and Sudan. In 1965 the population of Somalia was three million. Today it's above eleven million. In Sudan (including South Sudan), the 1965 population was twelve million. Today it's around fifty million (see Figure 4).

For all three countries, the population has almost increased by a factor of four from 40 million to 157 million in just fifty years. In comparison, the combined population of Britain, France and Germany only went up from 180 million in 1965 to 211 million today – a rise of just seventeen per cent.

There have been droughts in these countries in 1892, 1913, 1929, 1935, 1942, 1951, 1958, 1966, 1973, 1984 and 1998. It should be more than evident that three largely infertile countries that are regularly affected by drought every seven to ten years cannot successfully support a population that is increasing at such a rate. It's understandable why people in these countries have such large families. With a high level of child mortality, few jobs and no pension system, the only way for adults to ensure their future is to produce a large number of children in the hope that some will survive, get jobs and provide for their parents in old age. But what is logical for many millions of individuals has been a catastrophe for their countries.

Unfortunately, foreign aid's success in preventing child deaths and starvation in these countries has not been accompanied by a culture change that would lead to a reduction in family size. Yet when regularly appealing for our money to help with the latest crop failure and famine in these three countries, charities and aid agencies seem to forget to tell us about how fast these countries' populations are actually growing and that, however much money we give, these countries will continue to experience droughts and famines because the land is simply unable to support the increasing numbers of people living there.

Quote: *By 2050, the population of Ethiopia will be 177 million; the equivalent of France, Germany and Benelux today, but located on the parched and increasingly protein-free wastelands of the Great Rift Valley. So, how much sense does it make for us actively to increase the adult population of* *what is already a vastly over-populated, environmentally devastated and economically dependent country?*

But the problem is worse than just insufficient food. Too many people competing for too few resources - land, livestock, grazing grounds, water, mineral wealth, foreign aid - inevitably leads to conflict for those resources. And as these countries are made up of several distinct tribes, that conflict is usually tribal, brutal, extremely destructive and prevents any kind of economic or social development. In fact, conflict further impoverishes these and many other African countries.

In Sudan there has been a civil war between Sudan's various tribes for over thirty years. This tribal conflict should have ended in July 2011 when South Sudan became an independent country. There were joyous celebrations attended by the great and the good from the UN and we were assured that this split would at last give the Sudanese the chance to live in peace. Sadly the peace didn't last too long. First there was low-level war between Sudan and the new country of South Sudan. Then around the middle of December 2013 (about eighteen months after independence) the country's leader and opposition leader decided to fight over South Sudan's land, water, oil wealth and international aid money. So, an armed conflict broke out between the Dinker and Nuer tribes and, at the time of writing, there seems no reason this internecine slaughter will ever stop more than temporarily.

In contrast, by introducing its 'one child' policy, so widely criticised by liberal opinion-formers and *bien pensants* in the West, China managed to ensure that economic growth exceeded population growth and thus broke free from the poverty trap to set the country on the road to growing prosperity. In just a few decades, almost seven hundred million Chinese were taken out of extreme poverty. This has put China in a position where it can now consider relaxing the 'one child' policy.

2. Controlling corruption

Perhaps the most politically and racially emotive issue with foreign aid is the extent to which our money is lost due to corruption. Charities and aid agencies don't like to talk about corruption. There almost seems to be a self-interested conspiracy of silence amongst the lords of poverty around how much of our foreign aid is stolen by the elites in recipient countries. One can understand the aid agencies' reluctance to admit the existence and extent of corruption. If the public knew the true scale of venality, then this might sorely test our generosity and the generosity of our grandstanding politicians. So the attitude of charities and aid agencies seems to be that it's better to keep quiet about corruption in order that some aid gets through to the impoverished and destitute rather than risk little to no help reaching them at all.

Quote: *The dilemma faced by international organisations? If the robbers are not given their cut, they will not let the shipment of aid get through and the starving will die. Therefore you give the chieftains what they want, in the hope that at least the leftovers will reach those suffering from hunger[54].*

There are wildly differing estimates of the amount of aid money lost due to corruption. Around a third of all the aid sent to parts of the Balkans was given directly to Serb militias in return for permission for aid agencies to use roads in areas controlled by the Serbs. About two thirds of the aid given to Somalia between 2000 and 2010 was stolen or diverted to various warlords and their private armies.[55]

The scale of graft can be massive, even in countries which are not ruled by warlords. Millions of dollars were given to South Africa to buy schools textbooks. Hardly a single book was bought as almost all the money was allegedly stolen by people with close links to the ruling ANC Party. The year before the 2014 Ebola outbreak, $60 million of EU taxpayers' money was donated to Liberia to build clinics and train health workers. Of this $60 million, only about five per cent ($3 million) ever reached the Liberian Ministry of Health. At the time of writing, it wasn't clear what had happened to the missing $57 million.[56] A few months later, Liberia was the African country with the highest death rate from Ebola, partly due to a lack of clinics and lack of trained staff. And following the Asian tsunami in 2004, customs officers in Sri Lanka impounded vehicles and medical supplies we sent to help Sri Lanka's 516,000 displaced tsunami victims and the families of the country's 35,000 dead. The corrupt customs officers would reportedly only release the vehicles and aid in return for an immediate payment of around $1 million in cash bribes and further payments of another $2 million, again in cash.

The stories are almost endless. But we seldom hear them because, if the public knew how much of our money was being pillaged, then we might be rather less inclined to hand over our cash when the next disaster strikes and the next charity comes calling.

In 2013 there was a scandal in Cambodia involving $20 million gifted to buy mosquito nets. Around $3 million was paid in bribes with two officials allegedly pocketing about $500,000 each just from this one project and the director of the country's National Malaria Centre possibly getting $351,000. The rest of the money was wasted because corruption led to the mosquito nets not being treated with insecticide so they had to be scrapped and replaced. Following this, Bill and Melinda Gates authored an article in *Policy Options* in which they wrote 'suppose small-scale corruption amounts to a two per cent tax on the cost of saving a life. We should try to reduce that. But if we can't, should we stop trying to save lives?'[57] Sadly, in too many countries there is widespread, not small-scale, corruption, this is significantly above the Gates's two per cent level and this is decimating development budgets and wrecking relief operations.

Corruption affects emergency aid and development efforts in two main ways. Firstly, aid money or goods are stolen directly through expropriation by warlords, the military or politicians or else money pours out through bribes, tricks like double invoicing and shoddy (or even non-existent) construction work on roads, schools or hospitals or payments for imaginary children and schools. Britain's Department for International Development, for example, proudly claimed that £388 million given to a programme to support children going to school in India had reduced the number of out-of-school children by five million. But an Indian government report found that at least £70 million of this money had been stolen having been allocated to children and schools that didn't exist.[58]

Secondly, if foreign aid money pays for basic public services such as schools and healthcare for the poor, then local politicians feel little obligation to use the country's own money to provide these services. Thus generous provision of aid can tempt them into avoiding paying any tax, embezzling their departments' resources or wasting their country's wealth on vanity projects like palaces, mansions, fleets of Mercedes or space programmes. In Pakistan, few if any of the many multi-millionaire politicians, their business cronies or top bureaucrats pay any tax, leaving it up to foreign aid donors to hand over more than $2.5 billion a year to provide services for the poor in

Pakistan in order to make up for rich Pakistanis' tax avoidance. And the ability of Africa's greatest kleptocrats to loot billions is legendary. Although, on one list of the top ten greatest former kleptocrats, African leaders only occupy two places (see Figure 5)

Figure 5 – The Top Ten former kleptocrats and the amounts they are estimated to have stolen from their countries[59]

1. Former Indonesian President Suharto	$15bn–$35bn
2. Former Philippine President Ferdinand Marcos	$5bn–$10bn
3. Former Congolese President Mobutu Sese Seko	$5bn
4. Former Nigerian Head of State Sani Abacha	$2bn–$5bn
5. Former Yugoslav President Slobodan Milošević	$1bn
6. Former Haitian President Jean-Claude Duvalier	$300m-$800m
7. Former Peruvian President Alberto Fujimori	$600m
8. Former Ukrainian Prime Minister Pavlo Lazarenko	$114m–$200m
9. Former Nicaraguan President Arnoldo Alemán	$100m
10. Former Philippine President Joseph Estrada	$78m – $80m

Source: Transparency International

This list doesn't include kleptocrats who are still in power and still busily emptying their countries' and the aid agencies' coffers. Some of these are featured in our YouTube video – *"Africa"* by David Craig.

Much of the worst kleptocracy seems to have happened during the Cold War. At that time, the US and Russia were happy to ignore the venality of any leaders who sided with them in return for their support. But since the end of the Cold War, quite a few former kleptocracies such as Indonesia, the Philippines, Yugoslavia and Nicaragua have started moving towards some form of democracy and previous levels of thieving are no longer tolerated. It's not obvious that the same process has happened to the same extent in Africa.

One way of assessing what effect corruption might be having on aid programmes in Africa is to look at how much money the political, bureaucratic and military elites are believed to siphon off for themselves each year in the countries where most looting occurs and how much these countries receive in foreign aid (see Figure 6)

Figure 6 – In many African countries, the elites are looting more money than the country receives in foreign aid[60]

Country	Looted/year	Aid/year	GDP/capita
Nigeria	$14.2bn	$1.8bn	$2,688
South Africa	$10.1bn	$1.2bn	$11.035
Sudan	$2.6bn	$1.0bn	$2,417
Ivory Coast	$2.3bn	$2.0bn	$1,475
Ethiopia	$2.0bn	$3.4bn	$859
Zambia	$1.9bn	$1.0bn	$911
Togo	$1.8bn	$0.3bn	$1,600
Rep. Congo	$1.5bn	$0.2bn	$675
Liberia	$1.0bn	$0.6bn	$900
Chad	$0.9bn	$0.5bn	$1,744
Total	$38.3bn	$12.0bn	

In the top ten 'lootocracies' - countries where the largest amounts of money are being looted by the ruling elites - the powerful are stealing about $38.3 billion a year while their countries are receiving around $12 billion in foreign aid. In almost all of these countries, it appears that more money is being looted each year than is being given in aid. The only exception seems to be the largest recipient of aid - Ethiopia. A cynic might suggest that Ethiopia's massive annual aid of around $3.4 billion a year is simply too much for the country's leaders to steal without somebody raising an eyebrow.

If these figures for the estimated level of kleptocracy are anywhere near accurate, then a part of the solution to the problems of poverty confronting many African countries could be international efforts to crack down on corruption rather than forever increasing foreign aid hand-outs.

Nigeria is probably the most egregious example of foreign aid being poured into a seemingly almost bottomless pit of corruption and where a reduction in the levels of theft would achieve much more for the country's prosperity than any increase in foreign aid, however generous, ever could. Just a thirteen per cent reduction in looting by the ruling, bureaucratic and business elites would give the country as much money as it receives in foreign aid each year.

Nigeria should be one of the richest countries on the planet. It has crude oil reserves estimated at 35 billion barrels – enough to fuel the entire world for more than a year. In addition, it has about 100 trillion cubic feet of natural gas. In theory Nigeria's 177 million population should be prospering in a country that in recent years has launched four satellites into space. It's estimated that about seventy million barrels of crude worth about $5.5 billion are stolen each year. Since 1960, Nigeria has received around $400 billion in foreign aid – equivalent to four Marshall Plans. Yet seventy per cent of Nigerians live below the poverty line of $2 a day, struggling with failing infrastructure and chronic fuel shortages even though their country produces more crude oil than Texas and the theoretical GDP per capita is $2,500 – almost $7 a day. It's estimated that since 1960 about $380 billion of government money has been stolen by Nigeria's rulers and their cronies in the bureaucracy, the military and business. In many parts of Africa there's a word 'wabenzi'. It means the 'people of Mercedes Benz' and refers to the rich politicians, bureaucrats and businessmen who have fleets of Mercedes-Benz usually paid for with money acquired corruptly. And now, due to widespread poverty and unemployment in what should be a rich country, Nigeria is falling apart and could soon descend into yet another civil war. But the aid agencies of the West continue to pour foreign aid into Nigeria while seemingly being more than reluctant to tackle the real reasons the country is descending further into poverty and imploding into armed conflict.

3. Managing the 'resource curse'

The 'resource curse' is also known as the 'paradox of plenty'. It refers to the phenomenon whereby countries and regions with an abundance of natural resources, especially minerals and fuels, or which receive large quantities of foreign aid, tend to have lower economic growth and worse development outcomes than countries with fewer natural resources or less foreign aid. There are several reasons why resources or large amounts of aid can end up being a curse rather than a blessing:

Dutch Disease' - A large inflow of money into one sector of a country's economy can push up a currency making other sectors less competitive, resulting in business closures and job losses. This is also called the 'Dutch disease'. In the Netherlands in the 1960s, discoveries of vast natural gas deposits in the North Sea caused the Dutch guilder to rise, making exports of all non-oil products less competitive on world markets. Similarly in Britain in the 1970s, when the price of oil quadrupled and it became economically viable to drill for North Sea Oil off the coast of Scotland, Britain became a net exporter of oil and the pound soared in value. But the country fell into recession as exports of other products became uncompetitive, businesses collapsed and people lost their jobs

Destroying local commerce – The sudden arrival of large amounts of free or subsidised food or mosquito nets or tents or medicines or other products from aid agencies can ruin the livelihoods of local farmers or small businesses which previously supplied that food or those products

Broken bond - In countries that are not resource- or aid-dependent, governments tax citizens who hope for public services and reasonably efficient and responsive government in return. This bargain establishes a political relationship between rulers and subjects. In poorer countries, whose economies are dominated by natural resources or foreign aid however, rulers hardly need to tax their citizens because they have a guaranteed source of income from resources or foreign aid disbursements. Moreover, the administrative infrastructure to collect taxes is often corrupt or doesn't exist. As a result, citizens are poorly served by their rulers and, if citizens complain, money from the natural resources or foreign aid enables governments to pay for armed forces to keep citizens under control. Countries whose economies are dominated by resources or foreign aid tend to be more repressive, corrupt and badly managed.

Quote: *In most functioning and healthy economies, the middle class pays taxes in return for government accountability. Foreign aid short-circuits this link. Because the government's financial dependence on its citizens has been reduced, it owes its people nothing.*[61]

Fuelling greed – Aid money can enable a country's elites to amass fortunes for their own luxuries rather than using the money for the welfare off the whole population. Moreover easy access to offshore tax havens provides opportunities for corrupt politicians, bureaucrats and military leaders to hide their wealth

Behavioural changes – Supplying aid may have short-term benefits in terms of fighting disease or saving people from starvation. But there may be longer-term negative effects. For example, in times of famine people will naturally flood into camps where there is food distribution. But this can lead to a failure to plant the next year's crops thus prolonging, rather than reducing, hunger. Moreover, some of the best-paid jobs in many underdeveloped countries are working with aid agencies. Hence educated and qualified people like teachers, engineers, doctors and others may find they can earn at least five times more working as a translator or guide for an aid agency than they can doing the jobs for which they are qualified

Conflict – Large amounts of available money, from mineral resources or foreign aid, can provoke conflict as different groups, factions or tribes fight for their share. In theory, foreign aid should help improve the economic condition of recipient countries' populations. This has already happened in many countries. But in others still caught in the poverty trap, an excess of foreign aid badly controlled can cause impoverishment either because of the dislocation between ordinary people and the ruling elites or due to conflicts for that aid. Thus aid poorly managed can actually lead to a lessening or even destruction of democracy and increasing oppression of the suffering majority by the lucky self-enriching minority.

Quote: *Countries are not poor because they lack roads, schools or health clinics. They lack these things because they are poor and they are poor because they lack the institutions of the free society which create the conditions for economic development. Aid has it upside down.*[62]

Even though we now understand some of the key elements that enable societies to develop – things like individual property rights, the rule of law, a balanced relationship between government and people – we continue to pour tens of billions a year into countries that lack any of these elements and then we are surprised when those countries become more, rather than less, aid-dependent. It may now be the case that those countries which could develop by benefitting from foreign aid are already doing so. This leaves a hard core of countries, many in sub-Saharan Africa, where massive amounts of aid are proving to be ever less effective in helping those countries' populations. In these cases, it may be a change of approach, rather than an increasing quantity of aid, which is needed.

Chapter 7

Time for real charity?

The Problems

There seems to be ample evidence that the whole charity and foreign aid industry is spiralling ever more out of control. In Britain some of the symptoms of increasing chaos in the charity sector include:

Too many – with more than 195,289 registered charities and over 191,000 unregistered charitable organisations employing more than a million people, the charity industry is far too large for a small country the size of the UK

Attention deficit – with so many charities fighting for our attention and money making thirteen billion 'asks' a year, massive effort is wasted by charities on advertising, direct mail, chugging and other fundraising activities as charities compete with each other to see who can shout the loudest and stand out from the heaving mass of other charities all keen to enlist our support

Noise level – with so many charities clamouring for money from us, charities have to resort to increasingly expensive techniques to make themselves heard above the noise level

Overlap – there are far too many charities working in similar or identical areas doing similar or identical things

Wastage – with so many charities duplicating, triplicating, quadruplicating and worse their activities, there is massive waste of money and effort in management, fundraising, administration and governance which is siphoning off billions of pounds each year away from real charitable activities and into sustaining a vast army of charity professionals, advisers, consultants, accountants and lawyers who seldom if ever come into contact with real charitable work

Insufficient mergers – there are a few laudable examples where charity bosses and trustees have managed put aside their own self-interest and *amour propre* and have merged. This has resulted in less money being wasted on management and internal administration and more money being raised and spent on genuine charitable activities. But the number of mergers has been almost infinitesimal compared to the number of charities operating in similar areas which could and should be merged

Fake charities – it's far from clear which charities are really doing genuine charitable work relieving suffering or poverty and which are campaigning or political organisations clothing themselves in the cloak of sanctity while doing little to nothing that looks, smells or feels like genuine charity

Exaggerated claims – the charities' and the Charity Commission's assertion that between £8.00 and £9.00 of every £10 spent by charity goes to real charitable activities is simply not credible. The real figure is probably nearer £5 out of every £10

Excessive pay – while pay at some of the larger charities is not ludicrously high given their size and complexity and while the 'charity discount' does seem to exist at many larger charities, pay at some smaller charities is totally out of kilter with their size, their resources and the number of people who work for them

No control – the Charity Commission does not have the resources to supervise, and therefore has completely failed to control, whether spending classed as 'charitable' in charities' accounts actually is charitable or not. Moreover, the accountancies used by charities seem to have 'counted the beans' but similarly failed to try to spot whether expenditure classed as 'charitable' actually has anything at all to do with genuine charity

Scope creep – many of the larger charities have strayed extremely far from their original missions and indulge in an ever-increasing range of activities that may have little or nothing to do with their underlying charitable purpose. This expansion of their remits requires charity bosses to keep hiring more staff, paying themselves more and is perhaps more gratifying for the bosses than the hard grind of working with the poor and disadvantaged

Politicisation – pressure put on the Charity Commission by New Labour has led to a virtual free-for-all where there is little to no control on charities shoving donors' money into political campaigning rather than genuine charitable work. It's unlikely that members of the public are aware just how much of their money is used for political rather than charitable purposes.

In the area of the developed countries' $5 billion a year emergency aid and $130 billion a year development aid, some of the major problems include:

Law of Diminishing Returns – after fifty years of massive foreign aid assistance, those countries that can be helped by traditional foreign aid spending are succeeding in creating rising prosperity for their people. But there remains a group of poverty-trapped countries for whom no amount of aid will have any beneficial effect on their development and may even contribute to their further impoverishment

Overpopulation – perhaps the greatest threat to the possible prosperity of most poverty-trapped countries is the speed of their population growth which far exceeds any possible economic growth and thus can only lead to decreasing average prosperity and often civil war as more people fight over limited resources

Corruption – in the poverty-trapped countries, aid seems to increase corruption, dampen development and encourage mass repression

Poverty lords' self-interest – the career, personal and economic interests of the lords of poverty have resulted in a conspiracy of silence whereby we are constantly lied to about how much foreign aid actually reaches the disadvantaged and how effective this aid really is. This tendency to flatter what, if anything, is being achieved by emergency or development aid is reinforced by holier-than-thou politicians, journalists and media pundits all eager to appear as champions of the disadvantaged

Political correctness – for the poverty-trapped countries political correctness has prevented an open and honest discussion of why some countries have failed to develop. This has hindered taking a more effective approach to helping these countries escape the poverty trap. For example, it has now been alleged that the reason the World Health Organisation was so late in announcing an emergency over the Ebola outbreak, despite urgent requests from its field workers, was the fear of upsetting the leaders of the countries hit by Ebola. There were thousands of unnecessary deaths as a result.

Competition – in too many poorer countries there are far too many charities and agencies operating, all falling over each other to promote their own programmes and the careers of their own staff resulting in competition rather than cooperation to assist the supposed targets of their efforts. Moreover, the presence of too many charities can overwhelm the local bureaucracies' ability to work with these charities to achieve the best outcomes for the poor, the hungry and the sick.

The solutions

Given these and other problems with the ever-growing charity and foreign aid industries, there are a number of actions that probably should be taken to improve the functioning of these industries and to ensure that more money gets spent more effectively on genuine charitable activities.

For the UK charitable sector, these could include:

Identify the type of charity – at the moment, when a charity asks us for money, it's difficult for ordinary people to know whether their donations will be spent on genuine charity work or on campaigning for whatever political or moral issue the charity's bosses have espoused that month or year. Moreover, when a spokesperson for a charity comes on TV or appears in other media to lecture us about how we should live our lives, we don't know if that charity ever does any real charitable work and whether it is actually voluntarily supported by any members of the public or whether it is just a fake charity – a campaigning group living off taxpayers' money handed over by financially-incontinent governments.

To resolve this, the Charity Commission could create say four or five types of charity with strict conditions as to how those charities raise and spend their money. For example, we could have a group of charities called 'care charities'. The criteria for qualifying as a 'care charity' could be that no more than fifteen per cent of revenue should be spent on administration, fundraising and management; no more than ten per cent could be used for strategy development, creating awareness and campaigning and a minimum of seventy per cent of revenue should be used for genuine relief of suffering or poverty. Instead of just being given a charity number, these charities could be given a 'Care Charity' number. Clearly there would be an incentive for charities to qualify as a 'care charity' as it's likely that approved care charities would attract the most money in public donations.

There could be a class of charities called 'campaigning charities'. These would be allowed to spend more than ten per cent of their revenue on awareness and campaigning. Any 'care charity' which spent more than ten per cent of its revenue on anything that looked like campaigning would have its 'care charity' status replaced by 'campaigning charity' status. This would make it more difficult for that charity to raise money from the public and would act as a strong inducement for that charity to retain its 'care charity' status.

There could also be a group called 'organisations with charitable status' (OCS). An OCS would be any organisation which has been granted charitable status but doesn't seek to raise money from the public.

Probably there should be one or two other groups, perhaps 'educational charities' and maybe one other group, possibly 'political charities'.

Then when a charity came asking for money or appeared in the media, it should be under an obligation to let us know whether it was a 'care charity', 'campaigning charity', 'educational charity', OCS or some other kind of charity. This knowledge would help us decide whether we want to contribute any of our money or our time and also whether we should trust what that charity is telling us

Cut the numbers – there are clearly far too many charities and their numbers need to be more than halved. Moreover, there are insufficient mergers and far too many charities working in similar areas all competing for our attention and all wasting massive amounts of money on duplication of effort. The Charity Commission should start to actively reduce the number of charities by taking such measures as:

'Ten out, one in' – instead of allowing up to twenty five new organisations to register as charities each week, the Charity Commission should create a waiting list for organisations wanting charitable status and only allow one new charity to be registered for every ten charities that close and leave the register

Encourage mergers – the Charity Commission should identify between a hundred and two hundred suitable candidates for merger each year and give those charities twelve months to either merge or present a credible business case why a merger would not be in the interests of those the charity was set up to serve

Get control – the Charity Commission is struggling just to prevent tax avoidance schemes registering as charities. But it has absolutely no oversight or control over how charities actually spend our money. Each year, under the Gift Aid scheme, HMRC passes around £1 billion to charities. If just one per cent of this Gift Aid money - £10 million a year – was retained by HMRC and passed through as extra funding to the Charity Commission, the Commission could use this money to hire around 200 auditors. Each auditor could have four main responsibilities: firstly to audit the accounts of perhaps twenty to thirty charities each to ensure that money supposedly being spent on 'charitable activities' was genuinely being used for that purpose; secondly to ensure that 'care charities' were keeping to the spending limits for administration, fundraising, management and campaigning to control whether those 'care charities' should keep their 'care charity' status; thirdly to monitor charity CEO and managerial salaries and to flag up to the Commission any instances where charity leaders seem to be getting excessive rewards given the size of the organisations they were running and fourthly to identify possible targets for merger. In the short-term, this would obviously remove £10 million from charities' coffers. But by imposing some external control over what charities were doing, it should quickly discourage administrative profligacy, waste and duplication and very soon raise much more for real charitable activities than the £10 million per year cost.

'Traffic signalling' – on all their communications, charities could have a simple 'traffic-signalling' diagram – perhaps a small column or circle with just three colours – red for the proportion of revenue spent on administration, management, research and fundraising; amber for the proportion spent on campaigning and creating awareness and green for the proportion spent on genuine charitable activities. This would be controlled by the 200 extra auditors joining the Charity Commission and would give ordinary members of the public a quick and easy way to judge whether that charity deserves their support.

With foreign aid, some ways to improve the results achieved from the donor countries' $135 billion a year might include:

Single channel coordination – in some Third World countries, charities and aid agencies are clambering over each other in a rush to do what they think that country needs. Instead the donor countries should appoint one charity or agency which had prime responsibility for organising and controlling all charity and aid work within each country. This single point of coordination could ask any charities or agencies to carry out the actual aid, but it would avoid wasteful duplication whereby many charities all have their own expensive operations in the world's most deprived countries.

Conditionality – one option to try to force the failing poverty-trapped countries to reform could be to impose conditions for receiving aid. For example, the donor countries could create say three levels of aid. Level 1 would be emergency aid available to any country suffering a major famine, war, earthquake or other disaster. Level 2 could be help to build schools, hospitals, roads, clean water supply and other basic infrastructure and would be dependent on that country meeting various targets in how it spent its revenues and agreeing to an external body controlling any transfer of money above perhaps $100,000 out of that country. Moreover, no citizen of that country would be allowed to hold a bank account in a foreign tax haven. Level 3 might be assistance in power supply, sanitation, universities, house-building and agriculture providing that country had an effective programme of population control, a democratically-elected government and at least one peaceful change of government. Obviously, this proposal needs more careful thought about how it would work in practice. Nevertheless with a structure like this, recipient country governments would be absolutely clear about what was expected from them in return for receiving aid and their people would know why their countries were or were not receiving higher levels of aid.

UN protectorates – with too many countries, particularly in Africa, are caught in a vicious downward spiral where excessive corruption leads to impoverishment leads to rapidly growing populations (as families try to provide for their future) leads to further impoverishment it's possible one might consider extreme measures. Onel way to break this would be to start making some countries UN protectorates. With these UN protectorates, the UN would send in people to run the countries' civil services, health systems, education systems and development programmes until those countries were put on a path of growing prosperity. This ideal is probably impossible as it would look too much like recolonization. Moreover, the ruling elites, fearing a loss of opportunities to enrich themselves, could easily start campaigns of violence against UN administrators. Though it would be interesting if a few of these poverty-trapped countries could be given a democratic vote as to whether they wanted to stay as fully independent state under local rule or else become UN protectorates. One could suspect that many would prefer UN protectorate status and the benefits that would bring.

Conclusion – Our charities need to be more charitable

These suggestions are just intended to be a starting point. There are surely many more actions that could and should be taken to improve the results achieved from the money we give in charity and aid either directly from personal donations or indirectly from our governments handing over massive amounts of our tax money.

But hopefully this book has shown that the charity and foreign aid industry is out of control, risks becoming increasingly self-serving and delivers insufficient outcomes for the vast amounts of money given supposedly for the benefit of those who are the targets of our charity and foreign aid activity.

This book is not meant to be an attack on charity. But it is intended as an attack on many charities that put their own interests before the interests of those they claim to be working for.

Many charities and aid organisations have become hungry monsters needing ever more of our money to feed their own ambitions. It's time to get control of them, cut them down to size and refocus them on those they should be helping.

[1] *The Role of the Charity Commission and "Public Benefit"* Public Administration Select Committee May 2013

[2] Fundraising Standards Board Annual Report 2013

[3] *Independent* 28 May 2012

[4] *Guardian* 12 August 2011

[5] *Guardian* 30 April 2013

[6] *DYING OF MONEY Lessons of the great German and American inflations* Jens O. Parsson (Dog Ear Publishing 2011)

[7] *Sock Puppets* Christopher Snowdon Institute of Economic Affairs

[8] Charity Commission website September 2014

[9] Relate Annual report 2013

[10] *Daily Telegraph* 23 June 2012

[11] *The Role of the Charity Commission and "Public Benefit"* Public Administration Select Committee May 2013

[12] *Guardian* 8 August 2013

[13] *Report of the Enquiry into Charity Senior Executive Pay* NCVO April 2014

[14] *CEO Salary Debate* Christian Aid

[15] *Third Sector* 11 August 2014

[16] *Daily Telegraph* 17 January 2012

[17] *Fun London News* 30 July 2014

[18] *BBC* 5 July 2002

[19] Recruitment ad for street charity fundraisers (September 2014)

[20] *DON'T BUY IT Tricks and Traps Salespeople Use and How to Beat Them* David Craig (Thistle Publishing 2013)

[21] *Fun London News* 30 July 2014

[22] *Sunday Telegraph* 22 December 2012

[23] *IoF statement on Channel 4 Despatches* 12 August 2014

[24] *Trusted and Independent* Cabinet Office

[25] *Fundraising.co.uk* 25 March 2014

[26] *Birmingham Mail* 25 January 2014

[27] PFRA website September 2014

[28] *Daily Telegraph* 17 January 2012

[29] *Birmingham Mail* 25 January 2014

[30] *Conservative Home* 16 June 2014

[31] *Daily Mail* 10 June2014

[32] *Daily Mirror* 11 June 2014

[33] *Daily Mirror* 11 June 2014

[34] *Pioneers Post* 13 September 2014

[35] *Daily Telegraph* 11 August 2014

[36] *Daily Telegraph* 22 August 2013

[37] *Daily Telegraph* 22 August 2013

[38] *Daily Telegraph* 21 December 2012

[39] *Daily Telegraph* 14 September 2013

[40] *Daily Mail* 14 September 2012

[41] *Daily Telegraph* 6 September 2012

[42] Centre for Economic and Social Inclusion 10 September 2012

[43] *Third Sector online* 5 November 2012

[44] *Sunday Times* 14 September 2014

[45] *Alcohol Concern* Annual report 2013

[46] *Guardian* 5 December 2008

[47] Cabinet Office Strategy Unit 2002 (p.8)

[48] Charity Commission 2005

[49] *Sock Puppets* Christopher Snowdon Institute of Economic Affairs

[50] Charity Commission website 31 January 2014

[51] *Central Lobby* PoliticsHome

[52] *Dead Aid* Dambisa Moyo

[53] Peter Botting 29 May 2012

[54] *The Shadow of the Sun* Ryszard Kapuscinski

[55] *The East African* 21 July 2012

[56] *Sunday Times* 5 October 2014

[57] *Policy Options* March 2014

[58] *Daily Mail* 1 January 2013

[59] Transparency International 2004 report

[60] Amount looted figures from 'The ONE Campaign'

[61] *Dead Aid* Dambisa Moyo

[62] Fredrik Erixon, ECIPE

Printed in Great Britain
by Amazon